# TRUE HISTORY

## A NEW HISTORY OF IMMIGRATION

# TRUE HISTORY

## A NEW HISTORY OF IMMIGRATION

**BY JACLYN BACKHAUS**

SERIES CREATED BY JENNIFER SABIN

**PENGUIN WORKSHOP**

PENGUIN WORKSHOP
An imprint of Penguin Random House LLC, New York

First published in the United States of America by Penguin Workshop,
an imprint of Penguin Random House LLC, New York, 2022

Text copyright © 2022 by Jennifer Sabin
Cover illustration copyright © 2022 by Steffi Walthall

Photo insert credits: Completion of the Transcontinental Railroad: National Archives
photo no. 594940; Affidavit from Chinese Father: National Archives photo no. 278671;
Jewish Refugees in Poland: World War I Collection (Library of Congress) LCCN
2021670925; Immigrants Waiting at Ellis Island: Prints and Photographs Division (Library
of Congress) LCCN 97501083; Mother and Daughter in Tenement Housing, New York City:
Lewis Hine, National Archives photo no. 523503; The Statue of Liberty and Ellis Island:
Carol M. Highsmith, Carol M. Highsmith Archive (Library of Congress) LCCN 2011632948;
John Lewis, Civil Rights Activist: Pete Souza, Records of the White House Photo Office,
National Archives photo no. 157649496

PENGUIN is a registered trademark and PENGUIN WORKSHOP
is a trademark of Penguin Books Ltd, and the W colophon is a
registered trademark of Penguin Random House LLC.

Visit us online at penguinrandomhouse.com.

Library of Congress Cataloging-in-Publication Data is available.

Manufactured in Canada

ISBN 9780593386125

10 9 8 7 6 5 4 3 2 1 FRI

Design by Sophie Erb

# CONTENTS

# INTRODUCTION
## A NOTE FROM PROFESSOR
## CHRISTOPHER SEBASTIAN PARKER

*Parker is a professor of political science
at the University of Washington.*

Immigration is a controversial subject in the United States. One side, Republicans, typically approaches the subject as a matter of law and order: They're for immigration so long as it's legal. The other side, Democrats, generally prioritizes human rights over law and order. As such, Democrats tend to embrace immigrants, be they "legal" or not.

As Jaclyn Backhaus's *A New History of Immigration* illustrates so well, the controversy over immigration isn't new. In fact, it's been around for quite some time. In this book, Backhaus moves the narrative away from the "nation of immigrants" myth in which immigrants leave their

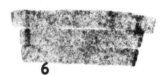

"old country" in search of prosperity in America. When immigrants arrive, Backhaus shows, they're often met with social hostility, and forced to experience economic hardship. Indeed, Europeans, Mexicans, and Asians—those who arrived prior to 1965—all faced a tough road, one filled with discrimination of all kinds. Needless to say, the reality was far from the utopia that immigrants imagined when embarking on their journey. Yet, this is where the similarities end. The road to American citizenship varies significantly, depending largely on one's country of origin, but this is mainly a substitute for race. European immigrants have had an easier path to citizenship than Asian and Latinx immigrants.

The pattern began with the Naturalization Act of 1790. This legislation restricted legal immigration and citizenship to only white men arriving from Western Europe. People with roots elsewhere, who were not free white persons, weren't allowed to make their new home in America. Next was the Chinese Exclusion Act of 1882, passed because the Chinese were thought by whites to be "unassimilable." In other words, they believed the Chinese too culturally "backward" to become part of American society. This law banned immigration from China for ten years, and this was *after* Chinese immigrants helped to build the Transcontinental Railroad connecting the East Coast to the West Coast. The immigrants received lower pay than whites, and were stuck with the most dangerous jobs. In fact, over one thousand of these workers died by the time the project was completed. After immigrants from Japan began to migrate to the United States, the Immigration Act of 1924 was passed, setting strict quotas on immigration. This all but stopped immigration from Asia for forty years. This is to say nothing of Japanese immigrants already in the United States prior to the Immigration Act who were forced into concentration camps during World War II when their loyalty was questioned on account of their ancestry.

When it comes to the Latinx community, primarily Mexicans, the origins are obviously different, but they suffered a similar fate to Asian immigrants. Prior to the Mexican-American War (1846–1848), Mexico encompassed, in whole or in part, Arizona, California, Colorado, Nevada, Oklahoma, Texas, New Mexico, and Utah. After the war, which was inspired by the doctrine of Manifest Destiny, Mexico was left with roughly half of its territory intact. Gone were all of the states just mentioned. Though the American government followed through on its promise to pay $15 million, it never honored its commitment to extend citizenship to those Mexicans stuck on the "wrong side" of the border when it crossed them. Nor did it (the American government) honor their property, their rights, or their culture.

Immigrants for whom the "old country" was Europe had a rough start, too. Benjamin Franklin had no use for German immigrants, the Irish faced religious and ethnic discrimination, as did the Italians. Of course, Jews faced "racial" discrimination on account of how they were treated in much of Europe: as an "inferior and dangerous race." However, over time, each of these groups worked hard to become white. Eventually, each would come to be accepted as equals in American society.

For non-European immigrants and their descendants, things haven't changed much. Of course, the Immigration and Nationality Act of 1965, the law that removed quota-based immigration for all groups, flung open the doors to American citizenship. That said, consider how the Latinx community, all *presumed* "illegals," continues to suffer from discrimination. As recently as 2010, Arizona passed a law that permitted law enforcement to ask "suspected immigrants" for proof that they were in the United States legally. Let's not forget the spate of anti-Asian violence against legal residents that continues to sweep the country.

What accounts for such different treatment? Why were European immigrants eventually accepted, and Latinx and Asian immigrants not? Why do the latter groups continue to suffer? The answer is simple: It's all tied to race and racism. For lack of a more suitable term, European immigrants can pass as white; immigrants from elsewhere cannot. Whiteness is the cultural baseline; everything else is considered the cultural "other."

In *A New History of Immigration*, Backhaus recovers the humanity of immigrants. She does so, in part, by preferring the term "Global Majority" to the more oft used "aliens" to refer to groups of people (non-whites) who leave their country of birth hoping to make a life elsewhere. Referring to this population as aliens, Backhaus suggests, emphasizes difference, reinforcing the sense of "otherness" they feel. By identifying this group as part of the Global Majority, she makes clear that, in fact, non-whites aren't alien at all: They're part of the majority.

Another way in which Backhaus recovers the humanity of immigrants is to draw on her own history. The book opens with her personal experience as a descendant of immigrants and closes by taking a look back at her ancestry. Her family history dates back to 1917 with her maternal grandfather's arrival in the United States from India. He eventually settled in Northern California, and started a family with another immigrant from India. In fact, Backhaus is able to trace her family's history in the United States to immigration legislation mentioned earlier.

Again, if the current political climate is any indication, immigration will continue to be a source of division in the United States for the foreseeable future. This book is indispensable in that it adds layers of much-needed reality to the myth of American immigration. For European immigrants, the myth becomes reality. However, if one's national origins lie beyond Europe, the myth is a lie.

# "THE CONVERSATION"

It's a conversation that I've had many times since high school, usually with someone whom I've just met. The conversation seems, on one hand, well-meaning and innocuous. And yet since those early days, I always feel an acute sting while having it.

The conversation goes something like this:

The person whom I've just met will make small talk to inquire a little more about me.

"So where are you from?" they'll ask.

"Arizona," I reply.

"Oh," they say, seeming a tad unsatisfied with the answer.

They try again.

"What about your parents? Where are they from?" they ask.

"My mom is from California, and my dad is from New Jersey," I reply, becoming aware of an angle to the inquiry.

"Ah," they reply. They pause, then, before reframing their question with a bit more specificity. "I was wondering more about where they're from *ethnically*."

"Ethnically?" I say, as though I've never been asked before.

"Like, where are they *from* from?"

"Oh."

Depending on who they are, if I feel I can trust them, I tell them my story. My mother's parents were immigrants from Punjab, a province in South Asia that straddles the border of India and Pakistan. My father's parents were immigrants from Germany. Usually, at that point, the asker is satisfied with the answer. Perhaps I will receive a small "wow" at the revelation of my parents' interracial marriage, which would have been illegal until 1967, when the Supreme Court ruled in *Loving v. Virginia* that bans against interracial marriage violated the Fourteenth Amendment of the US Constitution. But at the end of it all, the conversation leaves me with a feeling of otherness. By implying that I am not "from" Arizona—that because I look a certain way, I must be "from" somewhere else. The conversation seems to suggest that I do not "belong" here in my home country—the country where my family immigrated in the early half of the twentieth century.

Maybe you feel that way, too. Maybe "the conversation" makes you feel othered, or just annoyed. The irony is that so often the people who are asking those questions are also the descendants of immigrants. Because so many Americans are.

# CHAPTER 1
## AMERICA: A NATION OF IMMIGRANTS?

The United States of America has long been touted as "a nation of immigrants." This phrase is often used to describe how our country is mostly made up of citizens who are not native to this land—meaning that they, or their ancestors, arrived here as immigrants. Maybe you've heard this phrase used before in political speeches or overheard it in conversations between friends and family. You may have even read it in books. The phrase became popular back in 1958, when John F. Kennedy, then a senator from Massachusetts who could trace his family roots to Ireland, published an essay that later became a book with the same title, *A Nation of Immigrants*. In his book,

Kennedy argued that the United States is at its best when it remains a safe haven for immigrants and refugees.

It may (or may not) come as a surprise to you to learn that when he published the book, this was an unpopular argument to make. And to many people today, that argument is still unpopular. Ultimately, Kennedy's book was a success, and it would help pave the way for the senator to become the thirty-fifth president of the United States in 1961. Though he was assassinated in November 1963, *A Nation of Immigrants* would help lay the foundation for the Immigration and Nationality Act (INA) of 1965, which aimed to remove discrimination in the United States' immigration policy. But, as you'll soon learn, despite the act's ambitious intentions, it did not effectively end discrimination against immigrants— even today.

Beyond Kennedy's proclamation of America as "a nation of immigrants," there have been other words and phrases used in an attempt to describe the vast population of peoples living in the United States—phrases like "melting pot" and "patchwork quilt," for example. Regardless of which phrases you may have heard, each implies a similar sense of the joining together of different ingredients or threads to make a more unified whole. The way all of America's inhabitants, with their different cultural and social habits, contribute to a greater, stronger, and richer American fabric.

Consider our country's name: the United States of America. Fifty states that are stronger together than separated. In 1776, when the original thirteen colonies joined together, declaring their independence from British rule, each colony and its people—most of them immigrants from Great Britain, or their direct descendants—came together as one.

But words are powerful, complicated, and at times, insufficient. Ask yourself this: Does the phrase "a nation of immigrants" speak to each one of America's 332 million residents? Do Native Americans, the Indigenous people of this land, consider themselves included? What about today's descendants of enslaved Africans who were kidnapped from their homelands beginning in the 1600s and brought to this land against their will? The answers to these questions are complicated—just like the issue of immigration and its processes.

Some of the stories in this book will undoubtedly portray uncomfortable and difficult situations, or as some historians, like Hasan Kwame Jeffries, call it, "hard history." Hard history is made up of the stories that are often left out of textbooks. That's because much of history is written through a selective, nostalgic lens—meaning that it focuses only on the good parts while ignoring the bad parts. Take the very founding of our country, for example. You probably learned that Christopher Columbus "discovered" America in 1492, and for that feat, he is a hero. While Columbus's role in the shaping of the Americas and the world was surely monumental, the full history of his story is one filled with colonization and genocide—the deliberate destruction of a group of people. In this case, the Indigenous people of the land we today call America. When considering this fuller context, it's more complicated to call Columbus a hero, isn't it? This is hard history.

In this book, we will not shy away from this hard history. In fact, we will confront the legacies of violence, hatred, bigotry, white supremacy, oppression, and systemic racism head-on so we can better understand how we might combat them. These histories will touch on stories from people who can trace their lineages to all over the globe. And perhaps they will echo or represent stories from your own lineage. We will spend time looking at the early settlers from Germany,

Ireland, and Italy—who were not as warmly welcomed as you might think.

We'll learn about the importance and power of words surrounding the current immigration debate. For example, how the word *immigrant* is different than the word *refugee*. We'll also look at the history of our fluid and oft-changing borderlands and learn about the people from the Global South who seek to cross our borders today. And we'll hear immigrant stories from East Asia, Southeast Asia, and South Asia and learn about how the American civil rights movement helped pave the way for their welcoming. There is so much more ground to cover on the topic of immigration in America than we have the pages for, but our hope is that you end this book with more context about how our history informs the present moment.

First, let's look at the earliest years of the country's founding and the moments that led up to the signing of the Declaration of Independence. This will give us the proper foundation to begin understanding who we truly are as a nation. Then we can begin to look more closely at the phrase "a nation of immigrants," its political origins, its problematic status, and its hopeful promise.

## II. A Brief History of America's Founding and Philosophy

Beginning in the late sixteenth century, the first European settlers arrived on the shores of what is now the East Coast of the United States. Throughout the seventeenth century, more Europeans would continue to arrive, settle on the land, and establish their own colonies (despite the fact much of the land was already inhabited by Indigenous people).

You may have heard of the Pilgrims, a small group of Puritans from England, who in 1620 came across the Atlantic on the *Mayflower* to establish Plymouth Colony in what is now the state of Massachusetts. For the next century, more British colonies would be settled on the Atlantic coast. These colonies were known as the thirteen colonies. By 1776, these colonies came together to declare their full independence from Great Britain by drafting the Declaration of Independence, a document stating all the reasons why they wanted freedom from the king of England.

In that document, there is one famous phrase that you likely have heard: "We hold these truths to be self-evident, that all men are created equal, that they are endowed by their Creator with certain unalienable Rights, that among these are Life, Liberty, and the pursuit of Happiness."

The men who crafted that document, known as the Founders, undoubtedly had great foresight and wisdom as they laid down their vision for their new country and established the protection of its citizens. But, as you'll soon learn, these men were hardly perfect. In fact, most of the men who are considered Founders also enslaved people and profited off slavery. This fact in itself might give you pause when considering why, then, had they written "all men are created equal" and that each person has the right to "Life, Liberty, and the pursuit of Happiness"? Surely they did not believe that an enslaved person in 1776 was entitled to the right of freedom.

Soon after the new country was officially established, waves of Europeans continued to arrive on America's Atlantic coast, each person seeking a new life, freedom, and a chance at happiness—the American dream. But with much of the land in these colonies having already been inhabited by the earliest Europeans and Indigenous people, these new arrivals would begin heading farther west to uncharted (at least to the new Europeans) lands. And in doing so, a new worldview was born: Manifest Destiny, the belief that expansion throughout the United States was not only justified but inevitable.

### III. Manifest Destiny

The term was coined in 1845, and many of its advocates believed that they were destined by God to spread democracy across the country. The idea of Manifest Destiny can be traced further back to a white, European colonialist mentality set down by the earliest colonizers. After Cristoforo Colombo—or as most Americans know him, Christopher Columbus—arrived on charter from the Spanish royal family to the Caribbean and began to enslave Indigenous people and exploit the resources found there, Europeans developed the Doctrine of Discovery. What is this doctrine, you might ask? It is another ideology that predates and informs Manifest Destiny.

## WHAT'S THAT WORD:

An *ideology* is a system of beliefs and ideas. This system can inform things as large as theories held by entire societies, political parties, or cultures, or it can be as small as a personal belief. Ideologies can be the basis for people's actions. And, depending on what the ideology is, it can be helpful or harmful. Often historians reflecting on past events trace how certain ideologies might have impacted how those events occurred, and what they may have changed about society at large.

Elements of the Doctrine of Discovery date all the way back to the 1100s. The Doctrine of Discovery is used to justify the forced colonization and domination of lands that are not inherently Christian. Thus, the white Europeans' "discovery" of other existing and well-established cultures and societies in the Western Hemisphere, in both North and South America, did not mean that they were going to accept, celebrate, or attempt to learn from those societies. Rather, they were going to dominate them in the name of Christianity. Manifest Destiny is a concept that both described a particularly American version of the old Doctrine of Discovery and also foreshadowed the shifting borders of what we now call the United States.

## IV. America, the Land of Opportunity?

You may have heard that America is a place where "everyone" has a seat at the table, where people come for a better life

and better futures for their children. The United States of America has long been framed in books, films, and other cultural narratives as a "land of opportunity." But for the one million immigrants who arrive to the United States each year, this framing is a best-case scenario, meaning that this isn't the case for everyone.

These best-case scenarios are often not all they seem to be, though. For immigrants to the United States of America, to the land of opportunity, their experience are often different from their expectations. This has been true for every wave of immigration in our country's short history. In fact, the very idea of unity in these United States can be contested—beginning with our origin story and the language we use to describe the country's founding. For example, the use of the phrase *e pluribus unum*—that translates to "out of many, one"—does not derive from the notion of immigration. In more recent history, it is invoked to spark unity from Americans of all backgrounds and beliefs, but originally the phrase was used as a motto in 1776 by the thirteen colonies who collectively waged war for independence from the king of England. That war, the American Revolution, was won against the British on lands that were stolen from several

Indigenous tribes whose ancestral homelands comprised the entire eastern United States. Unity, togetherness, and oneness feel very far away when that context is considered.

Let's also look closer at the idea of America as a "melting pot." This phrase was first coined by Israel Zangwill, a British Jewish playwright who wrote a play in 1908 called *The Melting Pot*. Zangwill's title became a metaphor, or symbol, for America at large: that immigrants from all nations can arrive here and become Americans together. It is a notion filled, once again, with promise that together we can stand united. However, the phrase also contains a central problem. It hints at the notion of assimilation, the stripping away of identity in order to conform to a norm, often set in place by a known hierarchy (a system in which people are ranked and classified by status). In many ways, the phrase implies a potential loss of self, loss of identity, and loss of origin.

## WHAT'S THAT WORD?

*Assimilation* is the process or methods by which a group or culture adopts the values, beliefs, languages, and behaviors of the culture in power. Sometimes this process occurs voluntarily; other times, it's by force. Methods of assimilation can be conscious decisions, like changing one's name to be more easily pronounced. Sometimes these methods are unconscious, like distancing oneself from community customs. Immigrants from each wave and era have dealt with assimilation in different ways. Assimilation isn't inherently bad, but when it is subjected upon a minority group, it can be traumatic when the people in that group are forced to suppress their culture and, in many cases, abandon their native language.

Almost 250 years since the United States fought a war for its independence from the British, we are enmeshed in a war of perspective and context on the very immigrants who come to our shores and our borders. As we work hard, vote, and advocate for better lives for ourselves as US citizens, our short memories are in plain sight as we let the plight of the immigrant become a politically debated issue. How, then, can we claim to be a nation of immigrants, when we are not giving our current immigrants the tools, resources, and support they need to thrive?

What happens when we remember that at some point,

perhaps, our ancestors arrived here with a similar hope as those who arrive here today? That the dangers and unknowns of arriving to a new place with hope and adaptability were likely part of our ancestors' experience?

And what happens, then, when we remember that not everyone who lives here is an immigrant or a descendant of an immigrant? The phrase "a nation of immigrants" presents an erasure of two key historical components that were vital to the founding and building of this country: the Indigenous tribes who were displaced by the arrival of the first settlers, and the kidnapped Africans who were enslaved and brought to this land by force.

## V. Origin of the Phrase

Roxanne Dunbar-Ortiz, historian and author of the book *Not "A Nation of Immigrants": Settler Colonialism, White Supremacy, and a History of Erasure and Exclusion*, looks at the phrase in the context of the times. Why did then-senator John F. Kennedy choose this title for his book? Was it because he himself was the descendant of immigrants? Or was there more to the story? Dunbar-Ortiz says it was because he wanted to turn a "negative into a positive," and secure his position as a potential candidate for president.

In the early 1950s, Ben Epstein, the director of the Anti-Defamation League (ADL), had reached out to Kennedy to support his cause. The ADL is a civil rights organization originally founded to combat antisemitism—discrimination or hatred against Jewish people. Epstein was concerned with rising cases of xenophobia, the hatred of people from other countries, in America. So Epstein tasked Kennedy to produce an essay that would place immigrants and immigration in a positive light and outline his vision for immigration reform. Kennedy's essay was a mainstream hit and would soon pave the way for the theoretical embrace of immigration as the heart of American life.

The politicization of immigration, it seems, was inevitable. And yet, what remains is the fact that immigrants are arriving in our country every day—many of them refugees and asylum seekers. They are real humans, with real stories and true histories. We hope to bring these stories into context with one another and to make connections among them, in an attempt to further unite the people of the United States.

## WHO'S WHO?

According to the human rights organization Amnesty International, a **refugee** is a person who flees their home country because they are at risk for serious human rights violations and their government cannot or will not protect them from danger. For example, in February 2022, Russia waged war on neighboring Ukraine, forcing millions of Ukrainians to leave their homeland. All refugees have a right to international protection.

An **asylum seeker** is a person seeking protection from serious human rights violations, but hasn't been recognized legally as a refugee. This person is awaiting a decision on their asylum, or protection. Seeking asylum is also a human right.

## VI. The Problem with "A Nation of Immigrants"

The phrase might give pause to groups of Americans who feel that these words don't actually represent them. Let's consider, first, the case of the Indigenous people who originally populated North America. When the earliest European settlers arrived on the shores of the continent, they did not find the land uninhabited. The land was home to thousands of tribes, tribal nations, and tribal organizations—each with their own specific languages, codes of law, cultures, and habitual practices. Over the next several hundred years, their tribal lands were forcibly, and often violently, taken from them.

While the European settlers organized their own Revolutionary War, they also began writing and enacting their own laws. Many of these laws were antagonistic, violent, or genocidal in nature toward Indigenous people. And in many instances throughout our nation's history, the forced migration of Indigenous tribes is well documented. Consider the Trail of Tears (1830–1840), a series of forced displacements in which roughly one hundred thousand Native Americans were removed from their homelands by the US government, leaving thousands to die along the way. What does it mean when people are moved from place to place against their will?

The European wave of arrival to North America, and the system of thought that resulted in the settlers laying claim to land that was not theirs, is part of a mindset, structure, and sequence of actions called settler colonialism.

The framework of settler colonialism gives us a specific lens as we look back on the early days of European arrival to North America. We are able to identify that, yes, perhaps those settlers did arrive because of religious persecution or violence in their homelands. But when they arrived, they exploited, stole, and claimed lands from existing inhabitants: Native Americans. Rather than working with existing tribes or learning their cultures and practices in order to find compromise, the European settlers and their larger colonizing force, the British Empire, learned their practices to benefit themselves, and then embarked on a campaign of genocide.

eliminating that group from existence or from a particular location. The word was coined in 1944 by a Jewish lawyer named Raphael Lemkin. Forty-nine of Lemkin's relatives were killed in the Holocaust, when Nazi Germany murdered over six million Jews between 1933 and 1945.

There are nearly six hundred Indigenous nations active and existing today, and the United States is still reckoning with the violence and harm enacted on Indigenous people throughout history. For a deeper look into this important history, you can read *Indigenous America*, another book in the True History series. The treatment of Indigenous people is another hard history, one that should be viewed in its full light so that future generations can stop repeating the mistakes of the past.

## VII. Enslaved Africans

Another group that is erased when we use the phrase "a nation of immigrants" is a group of people who are the backbone of this country's origin in capitalism: the enslaved Africans who were captured and sold in bondage to work in labor camps in the United States. Because they were moved against their will, forcibly and violently, they cannot be considered immigrants but rather victims of kidnapping and human trafficking. The phrase erases their history completely by either insinuating that they were immigrants or that they are not included as citizens of this country.

During the Reconstruction Era, the period after the American Civil War, many formerly enslaved people and their descendants found that living conditions in states where slavery was recently legal were dangerous. This spurred the Great Migration, another movement of Black people within the country, many from the South, toward seemingly more integrated states in the North. In these scenarios, we see something similar to the often-heard plight of the immigrant: someone who finds their place of origin unsafe to inhabit, who hopes for a better life for their children, and who strives to make it right by entering a new land of opportunity.

While these families' ancestors, and members of their immediate families, may have lived in bondage, they were striving for a fair, just, and equal life. That striving continues to this day as we reckon with societal inequity based in the roots of white supremacy (the belief that white people are the superior race), borne on this soil from the American project of enslavement. The foundation of America rests on purported values of life, liberty, and the pursuit of happiness. These communities, like so many others, had and continue to have to fight for America to uphold those values—to live up to the great American promise.

When we talk about immigration, it is important to set the scene for the landing place. Though two major groups, Indigenous people and the descendants of enslaved Africans, do not claim the mantle of immigrants, they are part of the foundation on which the country was built. As are the original settlers who, ignoring the existing foundation and framework of the land, laid claim to it in the name of discovery, ownership, and newness. These groups of people laid the groundwork for the founding of the United States. This is the land that newcomers from all over the world are arriving to.

## VIII. To Whom the Phrase Speaks

And yet, in all the pain of erasure, there is something inherently hopeful about the idea of America's promise. I live in Queens, a borough of New York City that is home to Jackson Heights, a neighborhood that was recently named one of the most diverse in the world. My Queens neighborhood,

Ridgewood, is a few over from Jackson Heights. When I leave my front door and walk up to Seneca Avenue, the main thoroughfare, I pass a Venezuelan restaurant that neighbors a Yemeni bodega. Farther down, I pass a Polish grocery, a German bakery, a Nepalese breakfast spot, and a Mexican restaurant. A few blocks away, a Colombian cake shop. A Dominican nail salon. A Korean nail salon. An Indian eyebrow-threading salon. An Italian grocer. This confluence of cultures speaks to a sense of thriving and intermingling, of symbiosis and merging. It seems as through the American promise is at work!

But it also speaks to the history and pattern of human movement. Behind each of these storefronts on Seneca Avenue are people, families, and stories. Perhaps their parents immigrated or their grandparents or great-grandparents did. Maybe they immigrated themselves. Some may have resettled here as refugees while others are asylum seekers. Some may be unable to return to their homelands. Others might still maintain ties to their home countries and are working to ensure the arrival of their families. Perhaps they are naturalized citizens, or they have their green cards, or they are undocumented (you will learn about these terms soon). And many are citizens by birth. Yet, undoubtedly, all their lives have been shaped and informed by US laws, for better or for worse. These laws may have welcomed them and their ancestors, or they may have attempted (or still attempt) to keep them out. And these laws, as you will soon learn, have a long history of evolving and devolving. What impact do those shifting laws have as generations of immigrants' descendants plant roots and attempt to thrive here? We will be exploring that and so much more in this book.

So, is America a nation of immigrants? A melting pot? A land of opportunity? Through the documented histories of immigration, we will look at where those phrases succeed—and where they fail. Together, we will seek to discover whether our country can keep the promise it made.

## LET'S TALK ABOUT IT

* Do you believe that America is a nation of immigrants? Why or why not?
* Do you think it's possible for any phrase to speak on behalf of all American people? Why or why not?

# CHAPTER 2
## THE POWER OF WORDS

*Immigration* is a big word—meaning it is loaded with history, context, and politics. If you were to ask ten people what they think about immigration, you would get ten very different answers. That's because each person has their own worldview and perspective. This is a good thing, but part of the reason there is so much debate around the subject of immigration, both nationally and locally, is because everyone has different viewpoints—making the issues and politics complicated.

The topic of immigration can be overwhelming. It is filled with historic dates, policies, and laws. But most importantly, the concept also holds millions of personal and individual experiences—an important and enormous aspect of the true history of the United States. It is easy to lose sight of the people who are central in this experience, especially if we have no known connection to them. When we are learning about immigration, it is important to learn the history because that affects the experience of those who are on the path of immigration today.

This topic might hit close to home.

Perhaps someone in your family is an immigrant to this country, and maybe you yourself are an immigrant. There are many ways that the laws and the history of immigration in the United States might have affected your experience—big and small ways. As you read this book, you might be able to forge connections between your experience as an American and the experience of the American immigrant.

Throughout the history of immigration in the United States, certain words have been employed in the discourse, with two aims. On one side, the aim is to welcome, unite, and bridge gaps. On the other side, the aim is to draw a line—to separate from, to exclude. To *alienate*.

In any great and divisive debate, the words chosen to illuminate one's points are chosen with purpose and intention.

When it comes to immigration, words matter.

For example, let's talk about that word, *alienate*. Merriam-Webster defines *alienate* as "to cause to be estranged: to make unfriendly, hostile, or indifferent, especially where attachment formerly existed." We can recognize the root word, *alien*, which often evokes imagery of little gray emojis with big black eyes, funky green UFO captains, Martians, and, of course, Baby Yoda. However, the word *alien* is also often employed when talking about immigration, with a precedent rooted in our country's history: The Alien and Sedition Acts were some of the first immigration laws passed in our country.

## A CLOSER LOOK: THE ALIEN AND SEDITION ACTS

The **Alien and Sedition Acts** were passed by Congress in 1798 when the public and government feared war with France was inevitable. The laws restricted the activities of foreign residents (aliens) living in the United States and greatly limited freedom of speech and of the press.

The definition of the word *alien* changes based on the context around the word. For example, in the case of the little green guys, Merriam-Webster uses this definition: "extraterrestrial: originating, existing, or occurring outside the Earth or its atmosphere." However, it also holds other meanings, for example: "not familiar," "different from what you are used to," and "too different from something to be acceptable or suitable." All those definitions hold ideas about difference rather than similarity.

Now let's look at the definition of *alien* in immigration law: the Immigration and Nationality Act defines *alien* as "any person not a citizen or national of the United States." The word *alien* may take on a new and specific meaning when it is used in relation to immigration, but that idea of difference, of apartness, cannot be untethered (separated) from the word in its other uses. When we think about aliens, we naturally think of a divide and something scary. Perhaps in our mind there is a notion of Us, and of Them.

When the Founders and the early US government wrote and signed the Alien and Sedition Acts in 1798, they were doing so from that same divide. They failed to see what their own settler colonist origins had in common with those folks attempting to move to the United States in the 1700s. Rather than seeing a connection between their arrival in once-foreign lands and the arrival of new neighbors, they chose to see difference. They decided that they were superior to those who came after them and were entitled to claim the country as theirs. In doing so, they chose a framework of exclusion that would continue to shape how immigration is perceived to this day. The word *alien* is still often used in conversations around immigration.

But there are signs of change. In April 2021, the United States Citizens and Immigration Services announced that they would be removing the word *alien* from their policy manual, in an effort to "use more humanizing language." Until then, the term was used in the manual 1,700 times.

Some of the new and more humanizing language includes the term *noncitizen*, as well as the phrases *undocumented noncitizen* and *undocumented individual* when referring to folks who do not yet have green cards or visas. Even the word *assimilation* will be replaced in the manual, with *integration* or *civic integration*. But there are plenty of people in government who still like to use words with more negative connotations, especially the word *illegals*, which we'll discuss soon.

When we use the word *humanize* in reference to someone, we mean that we are portraying them in a way that emphasizes, rather than reduces, that person's individuality or personhood. The practice of using more humanizing language is happening in many arenas of historical conversation, including those around enslaved Africans and the American incarceration system. For example, rather than call people *slaves*, we call them *people who are enslaved*. Rather than call people *prisoners*, we call them *people who are imprisoned*. They are people first. The difficult conditions of their lives come second, and it is not the only thing that defines them. The language often used to describe people can in fact dehumanize them—in other words, some terms end up objectifying them, condemning them, and reducing their worth. By humanizing the language that we use, we can continue to build bridges and reduce harm.

## THE FOUR TYPES OF IMMIGRATION STATUS

It will be useful to chart the different terminology that refers to immigration status, as these words are used in history and also are active in immigration conversations going on now.

1. **Citizens** are people either born in the United States or people who have become naturalized citizens, typically three to five years after becoming US residents.

2. **US residents** fall into two basic categories:

(a) **Conditional residents** are those who, within two years of marrying a US citizen, are able to receive their government-issued permanent resident cards (often called a "green card" because the original version of the document was a greenish hue), and

(b) **Legal permanent residents** are those who have obtained their green cards and are able to permanently live and work in the United States.

3. **Nonimmigrants** are people who are living and working in the United States but only temporarily. For example, some students, employees, and tourists hold special visas and are considered nonimmigrants.

4. **Undocumented immigrants** are people who have not obtained legal paperwork to live and work in the United States, either by overstaying nonimmigrant visas or entering the country in an unauthorized way and neglecting to enter through a port of entry.

## II. Power of Words in Action

In 2010, the nonprofit organization Race Forward began a campaign called "Drop the I-Word," which called for a language change in national and global publications to reduce dehumanizing language around undocumented immigrants. The i-word in question is *illegal*. For decades, this word shaped the narrative of immigration. It was often joined with the word *alien* to create the term *illegal alien*, which meant that prejudices of both unfamiliarity and criminality were identified with a person before their story was heard. In the land of America, where we are told we are innocent until proven guilty, using the term *illegal* is a premature judgment outside of a court of law. It is another example of dehumanization.

Top journalists around the country tend to agree. Race Forward says that since the start of their campaign, uses of the i-word in major publications like the *New York Times*, the *Washington Post*, and the Associated Press (AP) have declined. In fact, the AP even addressed the idea in its stylebook (a guide that details which words writers should use), stating it no longer condoned the use of the i-word and that illegal "should describe only an action," not a person. The conversation is ongoing, and in more inflammatory rhetoric, the word is employed. But more and more journalists are turning to the use of a new word: *undocumented*. This word implies not a criminal but a lack of paperwork—a potential, a hope, for a path forward. By laying out the data and the case for change, Race Forward was instrumental in the fight to strip a harmful word of its power.

And the path forward could be bright for the entire United States. Recent studies by the Center for American Progress show that offering undocumented immigrants US citizenship could boost our country's economy by $1.7 trillion in the next ten years. In the meantime, those who are undocumented and live in the United States are unable to access health care through the government or have any security about their home. And only sixteen states currently allow undocumented immigrants to get a driver's license.

## WHAT'S THAT WORD?

*Naturalization* is the process that people undergo to become citizens of the United States. After meeting requirements established in the original Immigration and Nationality Act, passed in 1952, people can apply. Then, they will be interviewed, take a test, and upon receipt of approval, take an oath of allegiance to the United States at an official naturalization ceremony. These ceremonies are often full of excited new citizens celebrating with their families over food and cake. At one citizenship celebration this author attended, the table was covered in McDonald's chicken nuggets and french fries.

### III. Where Words Lead

We can trace the impact of the language we use and the effect it has on the communities it describes. Immigrant communities have been subject throughout time to different kinds of stereotypes, or negative and untruthful judgments or opinions. Many stereotypes are rooted in feelings of difference or separation between one group and another, or between one person and another.

## WHAT'S THAT WORD?

A *stereotype* is an oversimplified idea or image of a person or group, usually based on race, class, religion, gender, or cultural habits.

# COMPLETION OF THE
# TRANSCONTINENTAL RAILROAD, 1869

On May 10, 1869, the Golden Spike ceremony at Promontory, Utah,
commemorated the completion of the transcontinental railroad,
which linked the East and West Coasts of the United States. Although
Chinese immigrants made up 90 percent of the workforce, the laborers
were excluded from this photograph. Following the completion of the
railroad, anti-Chinese sentiment increased. Soon, the Chinese Exclusion
Act of 1882 banned Chinese immigrants from entering the country.

# AFFIDAVIT FROM CHINESE FATHER, 1909

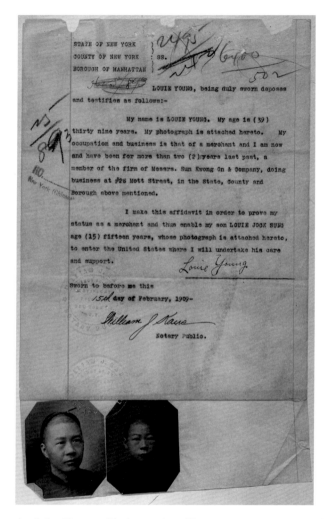

As a result of the Chinese Exclusion Act, Chinese immigrants were barred from entering the United States. In this document, an American-born Chinese man and father, Louie Young, testifies to prove his status as a merchant and to request that his son, Louie Jock Sung, who was born in China, be allowed to enter the country under his father's care. Many people in the Chinese community faced similar challenges and were denied US citizenship until the Chinese Exclusion Act of 1882 was repealed in 1943.

STATE OF NEW YORK
COUNTY OF NEW YORK
BOROUGH OF MANHATTAN

LOUIE YOUNG, being duly sworn deposes and testifies as follows:—

My name is LOUIE YOUNG. My age is (39) thirty nine years. My photograph is attached hereto. My occupation and business is that of a merchant and I am now and have been for more than two (2) years last past, a member of the firm of Messrs. Sun Kwong On & Company, doing business at #28 Mott Street, in the State, County and Borough above mentioned.

I make this affidavit in order to prove my status as a merchant and thus enable my son LOUIE JOCK SUNG age (15) fifteen years, whose photograph is attached hereto, to enter the United States where I will undertake his care and support.

[Signed] Louie Young

Sworn to before me this
15th day of February, 1909—

[signed] William J. Kane
Notary Public.

# JEWISH REFUGEES IN POLAND, 1921

In the aftermath of World War I, widespread destruction, famine, and economic distress destroyed Europe, forcing millions of people to seek refuge elsewhere. In eastern Europe, civilians were particularly devastated after the Russian Revolution led to a civil war, causing widespread displacement. The Jewish refugees seen in this photo are in Równe, Poland (present-day Rivne, Ukraine).

# IMMIGRANTS WAITING
# AT ELLIS ISLAND, 1912

A group of immigrants at Ellis Island stand with their bundles of belongings and suitcases, on a dock overlooking New York City. One can only wonder where they may have gone next.

# MOTHER AND DAUGHTER IN TENEMENT HOUSING, NEW YORK CITY, 1911

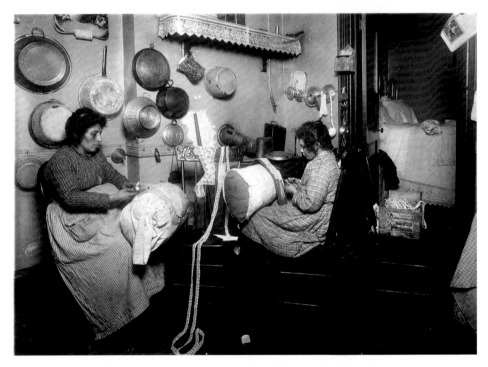

A woman, Mrs. Palontona, and her thirteen-year-old daughter stitching pillow lace in the kitchen of their small, shared housing unit. New immigrants like the Palontonas found shelter in tenement buildings that were overcrowded and under-resourced. Children often worked from a young age to help support the family.

# THE STATUE OF LIBERTY AND ELLIS ISLAND

Originally a gift from the French, the Statue of Liberty has become a literal and figurative symbol of America's promise: freedom and opportunity. Today, the statue is also a reminder of the plight of the millions of refugees who arrived in the earliest waves of immigration in the twentieth century. Ellis Island and its museum can be seen behind Lady Liberty.

# JOHN LEWIS, CIVIL RIGHTS ACTIVIST

The work of John Lewis cannot be overstated: His lifelong commitment to end systemic racism and inequality began in the 1960s and lasted until his final days as a US congressman before he passed away on July 17, 2020. Lewis's activism was instrumental in the passage of the Civil Rights Act of 1964. This set the stage for the passage of the Immigration and Nationality Act of 1965, which widened the road for Asian American immigration. In this photo, John Lewis is seen embracing President Barack Obama during a ceremony in 2015 commemorating the fiftieth anniversary of Bloody Sunday and the Selma to Montgomery civil rights marches.

These types of feelings are similarly evoked by the meanings of words like *alien*. As we visit different histories in coming chapters, we will see in many cases how those negative stereotypes affected lawmaking, separated communities and families, and kept the American promise at bay.

In his book *This Land Is Our Land: An Immigrant's Manifesto*, author Suketu Mehta combats three major stereotypes that have been construed about immigrant communities: that they commit more crime, steal American jobs, and refuse to assimilate into American culture. Mehta uses real-life research and his own power of words to undo harmful and unfair judgments that are often presented as fact. For example, many Americans believe that immigrants are more likely to commit crimes. Why? There are multiple reasons, but likely because they heard a politician say so. This is an inaccurate stereotype.

To debunk this, Mehta cites a 2016 study by Alex Nowrasteh of the Cato Institute (a research center), which found that in Texas "the native-born criminal conviction rate was . . . 2.4 times as high as the criminal conviction rate for [undocumented] immigrants in that year and 7.2 times as high as that of legal immigrants." In other words, immigrants are actually less likely to contribute to crime rates than United States–born citizens.

Another stereotype politicians often claim is that immigrants "steal" jobs from American citizens. Here, Mehta references a 2015 study by the National Academies of Sciences, Engineering, and Medicine that explains how this, too, is false. In fact, their presence in the workforce actually has positive effects. The study says "immigration is integral to the nation's economic growth."

Mehta, an immigrant himself who emigrated from India and moved to Queens when he was a young boy, writes firsthand of his experience not only holding on to his old culture but letting himself find joy in his new culture—and watching the two mesh and evolve into something bigger. He writes:

> [W]e were in a new country now, making a new life. And we could live side by side and interact in certain demarcated ways. We could exchange food; our kids could play together; they could go to school together. We discovered that we are more alike than different.

He also experienced racism growing up. Vandals would write slurs on his father's car, and schoolmates would hurl insults at him as he walked around campus. Mehta knows that while he experienced this in 1977, immigrants and communities of color still have similar experiences today. Part of the reason that he wrote *This Land Is Our Land: An Immigrant's Manifesto* was to try to define the immigrant experience in a way that is empowering to those communities, that humanizes rather than dehumanizes them. He wanted to showcase the impact that racism and white supremacy have on the immigrant but also offer the hope that they—and we—might transcend that hate, for the betterment of our country.

## WHAT'S THAT WORD?

To *immigrate* is to describe where a person *arrives* after they have moved.
To *emigrate* is to describe where they *moved from*.
For example, Suketu Mehta emigrated *from* India, but he immigrated *to* Queens, New York City.

## IV. The Global Majority

More recently, other writers and thinkers like Suketu Mehta have taken it upon themselves to craft new and empowering language for immigrants and communities of color to diminish the impact of racist language. One researcher and educator, Rosemary Campbell-Stephens, conducted work in London on leadership preparation in the early 2000s, and it was during that work that she coined the term *global majority*. She writes,

> Global majority is a collective term that first and foremost speaks to and encourages those so-called to think of themselves as belonging to a global majority. It refers to people who are Black, Asian, Brown, dual-heritage, indigenous to the global south, and or have been racialised as 'ethnic minorities.' Globally, these group currently represent approximately eighty per cent (80%) of the world's population.

In response to language that did not feel empowering across racial and community lines, Campbell-Stephens invoked the power of words. Instead of the term "people of color," which she argues "still situates [positions] whiteness as the norm," she offers the use of global majority to shift hierarchies and power structures. The term is now being used by young people, scholars, thinkers, teachers, and many other Americans as an empowering alternative to words that carry with them some of the stereotypes mentioned before.

Are all immigrants to the United States members of the global majority? No, and that has been true from our country's origin. But as we dig into some of these immigration histories in these next chapters, perhaps you will be able to draw connections between the hierarchies that existed in the early United States and the ones that exist now. Maybe you'll see a link between the unkind or welcoming words that met them upon their arrival to America then and now.

You might also be wondering: If there is power in the idea of the global majority, then why should people want to move to the United States? Why are people trying to come here in the first place, if difference and divide are represented in the language of their arrival? There are infinite reasons why.

## V. Infinite Reasons

Each person who strives to live in the United States has a different story. Those stories may start in tragedy, or they may start with joy. Each person at the center of their story may have lived through war, famine, poverty. They may have celebrated birthdays, weddings, and graduations. They have dreams, wishes, delights, and hopes for themselves. They have close loved ones, whom they want to provide for, care for, or save. They may have aspirations of attending universities, landing their dream jobs, getting a better education in elementary school. They may be survivors of domestic abuse, violence, or climate catastrophe. They may be moving for work, for love, for adventure. They are parents, children, spouses, and siblings. The choice to move away from a homeland is not an easy one. And in every story, sacrifices are made.

As we move through the rest of this history, you may find moments when you identify part of your culture or heritage, a small bit of your history in this country. Perhaps you do not feel "alien"—you just feel like you! But it's important to remember that this language of alienation, of exclusion, may have followed one of your ancestors. How do you think that made them feel? How might it have affected them?

The power of words is real. And when we recognize that power, we can shift to using language that is more empowering for everyone. This leads us down roads of connection and unity rather than isolation and harmful stereotypes. As you move through this book, continue to think about how you might be able to shift your relationship to the words you're reading, and to the images these stories lead to in your mind. How might you imagine early settlers as refugees of war? How might you look at what is happening at our southern border and see survivors and asylum seekers? Being able to choose how we use our words is one of the greatest powers we have. As we move into the next section, when we see other powerful forces and how they have shaped the very borders that come into the argument, we should remember that we hold power, too.

## LET'S TALK ABOUT IT

* Is there any immigration history in you or that you know of in your family? Who might you be able to ask, or what research might you be able to do, to find out more information?

* What does the phrase *global majority* mean to you? Does it feel uniting or divisive? Why?

# CHAPTER 3
## OUR BORDERLANDS

When you think of the word *immigration*, what image pops into your mind? The word is capable of evoking many different images, but one of the most prominent we see on television and in the newspaper is that of the southern border, where the United States meets Mexico.

You've probably seen some of the more upsetting stories on the news, the harsh way people are often treated when they come to the United States across the border from Mexico, especially during the Trump Administration (2017–2021). One reason families will risk everything is danger. People traveling from places like Honduras, a country that has become increasingly dangerous and deadly for many of its citizens, come to the border of Mexico and the United States as refugees, seeking shelter from those dangers.

You may have also heard about the child-separation policy instituted under President Trump in which children, some as young as babies, were taken from their parents when they crossed the border seeking asylum and were placed in detention centers away from their parents. Maybe you've learned about the politics always swirling around the border, with Republicans and Democrats often holding very different views about who should be let in and who should be kept out. President Trump, for example, campaigned on the slogan "Build the Wall" and used disparaging language to talk about immigrants coming from Mexico and Central American countries, sometimes calling them criminals. These political disputes have a long history. But often in those disputes, the plight of real people, especially children, seems to be overlooked. Here are just two (of the millions) of those plights.

## II. Nicki Minaj

Rapper and hip-hop superstar Nicki Minaj was born Onika

Tanya Maraj in the Caribbean country of Trinidad and Tobago. When her mother immigrated to the United States, Minaj was left in the care of her grandmother. Minaj and her brother Jelani were finally able to join their mother in New York when Minaj was five, settling in Queens. In 2010, Minaj described her arrival in the United States:

> I thought [the United States] was gonna be like a castle. Like white picket fence, like a fairy tale. I got off the plane and it was cold. I remember the smell. I could always remember the smell when I got out of the airport, of the snow, and I had never seen snow. I remember the house. I remember that the furniture wasn't put down. The furniture was, like, piled up on each other, and I didn't understand why, because I thought it was gonna look like a big castle.

Minaj found her footing in the hip-hop scene after moving to New York, and since her breakout debut album *Pink Friday* in 2010, she has become one of the best-selling recording artists of all time. In 2018, Minaj went public with a previously unknown part of her immigration story: When she came to the United States, she was undocumented. In response to President Trump's child-separation policy, she wrote in an Instagram post:

> I came to this country as an illegal immigrant at 5 years old. I can't imagine the horror of being in a strange place and having my parents stripped away from me at the age of 5. This is so

scary to me. Please stop this. . . . Can you try to imagine the terror & panic these kids feel right now? Not knowing if their parents are dead or alive, if they'll ever see them again . . .

Minaj was able to find community and thrive after arriving to the United States, after sacrificing time with her mother for the formative years of her childhood. By using her platform to voice her own lived experience, she was highlighting the plight of the children whose voices don't get heard in the debate. Minaj is just one member of a large and flourishing Afro-Caribbean diaspora in the United States— and the legacy of her music is only the beginning.

## WHAT'S THAT WORD?

*Diaspora* is a term used to describe people, or a group of people, who live outside of the place they consider their homeland. Indians make up the largest diaspora population, with eighteen million people living outside India but still calling the country their home.

### III. Valeria Luiselli

Valeria Luiselli is a Mexican author, educator, and parent who lives and teaches in New York. Her work, which stretches across fiction and nonfiction, often touches on immigration and immigration policy as it has morphed in the last twenty years. Her book *Tell Me How It Ends: An Essay in Forty Questions*, published in 2017, is a haunting portrait of child refugees, many from Central America, who embark on perilous border crossings only to arrive in the United States to face months or years of legal proceedings. The book is modeled after the forty questions in the intake test for unaccompanied child migrants, administered to children who have crossed the border upon their arrival to an immigration center. Luiselli volunteered as a Spanish translator in 2015 and administered this exam to several young people, all of whom knew little to no English. During her experience as a translator, she documented firsthand the struggles of the children who were not only leaving behind harsh homelands but also facing seemingly insurmountable odds of attaining visas, green cards, or other documentation. By writing the book, Luiselli is offering a glimpse into the plight of young people whose homelands are ravaged by dictatorships, gang violence, and climate disaster; who just want to play soccer, survive, and pave the way for their younger siblings to make the trek as well.

At the end of the book, Luiselli illuminates a positive outcome of her work. Students of hers at Hofstra University were motivated by Luiselli's stories of the children and teenagers she was meeting in her work, and they saw an opportunity to help. They started an organization called TIIA, which stands for the Teenage Immigrant Integration Association. TIIA's aim is to offer programming that serves new teenage arrivals to the United States, offering services like English classes, community discussions, and college-prep sessions, while also working with other immigration nonprofits to help with citizenship paperwork and more formal logistics. These young students heard the call to action and responded in a way that impacted several immigrants' lives, one by one, for the better.

## A CLOSER LOOK: THE FIGHT FOR DACA

In 2012, while Barack Obama was the US president, a new piece of legislation was introduced that offered protections for children who were living in the United States without citizenship or legal residency status. The program is called the **Deferred Action for Childhood Arrivals (DACA)**, and recipients of DACA status are often referred to as Dreamers, based on a previous law that created pathways to citizenship for young American hopefuls called the DREAM Act. Most current DACA recipients emigrated from Mexico, Central America, and the Caribbean. In the years since it began, DACA has been repealed, reinstated, and sanctioned several times. All the while, the original DACA recipients have grown from children to adults, and their constantly changing status makes it difficult for them to hold jobs, buy houses, or raise families without the threat of deportation. The fight for DACA rages on today—and at the center of it all are children, just like you, who hope they can keep the only home they remember and truly know.

## IV. The Border Today: ICE

We often see haunting images of border crossings in the news: detainment centers with a severe lack of amenities, where detainees are left to languish for months or years in facilities that are more like prisons than the friendlier word *centers*. Recently in Texas we saw US Border Patrol officers on horses, trying to wrangle Haitian refugees in a manner that evoked the history of slave patrols. Sometimes, the imagery leaves us hopeless, and we wonder if there will be any end to the dehumanization of these newcomers.

In order to situate ourselves in the immediate present, we must look at other key players in the current debate. One is Immigration and Customs Enforcement, or ICE, an agency created in 2003 that took over some immigration operations from the former Immigration and Naturalization Service. ICE is responsible for several immigration protocols, the most infamous being those carried out by its Enforcement and Removal Operations division. In previous years, according to the *New York Times*, ICE was mandated to focus its detention and deportation operations on "undocumented immigrants who had committed serious crimes." But in 2017, ICE was given permission to deport any undocumented immigrant from anywhere in the country. As discussed in Chapter 2, many undocumented immigrants are on the pathway to citizenship. They are applying for their green cards, raising families, and working to secure naturalization. This new proclamation put all those plans in jeopardy.

Another player is Customs and Border Protection (CBP), the agency that oversees the operations of the US Border Patrol, which monitors and regulates the southern border. In 2018, CBP met the ire of millions of Americans when it was discovered that the US Border Patrol was separating family members who arrived at the border. Parents and children, many of them asylum seekers from Central America, were forcibly detained and separated as part of their processing at the border. Photographs of isolated children, kept away from their parents in cages in cold warehouse rooms, evoked images of labor camps, of imprisonment. Children as young as five were separated from their parents, and a few children even died. Medical officials have since called such a practice a form of child abuse. Public outcry against this abusive practice sparked hundreds of protests across the country, including a protest in Atlanta, Georgia, that Congressman John Lewis attended. In June 2018, President Trump signed an executive order halting the practice that his administration had put into place only months before. But the damage was done. In 2021, it was estimated that thousands of children were still waiting to be reunited with their parents.

However, there are stories of hope amid the pain. There are many organizations that aim to ease some of the burden and assist those who want to make America their home. The Florence Immigrant and Refugee Rights Project, a nonprofit based in southern Arizona, works to provide legal aid to immigrants who are making the trek to the United States. Recently, they sent an update about one of their young clients, Mateo, who just turned eighteen and was released from government custody. The Florence Project's team of social workers and lawyers readied Mateo's case over several months while Mateo waited in a children's shelter. Upon his release, Mateo shared his dreams for the future: "In the future, I want to continue my studies and be my own boss. I'm not sure what kind of business. I want to have great experiences like you who are attorneys, and to help people. . . . Thanks to you, I could leave the shelter and have new experiences."

## V. History of the Border

Borders are something that we may think of as fixed, yet they are always changing. The continental United States—forty-eight contiguous states, excluding Alaska and Hawaii—borders only two nations: Canada to the north and Mexico to the south. The borderlands to the south currently stretch from San Diego, California, all the way to the easternmost tip of Texas, a city called Brownsville. The border follows the Rio Grande and other rivers to the Gulf of Mexico. But this has not always been the case. The southern border as we know it today is only about 150 years old. The way it is drawn now reflects wars, land purchases, colonization periods, imperialism, settlements, and negotiations. In the long arc of history, the borderlands are very new. And yet they are argued over and politicized as the front lines for today's immigration policies. Even as a young country, the US government had its hand in drawing and reshaping borders that would impact cultures and families all the way to the present day. The idea of movement and expansion, of addition and Manifest Destiny, kept the United States growing from a settler-colonial project to a world superpower. And our borderlands, as we know them today, were greatly impacted.

## HISTORY RECAP: LAND OWNERSHIP IN THE UNITED STATES

To understand the history of the shifting border, let's recap some of the ways that land ownership in the United States has shifted over time. England, France, and Spain all laid claim to various sections of North America west of the Mississippi River. Thomas Jefferson, the third US president, surmised that the entirety of the United States could stretch beyond the original thirteen colonies and extend into the West. In 1803, Jefferson orchestrated the **Louisiana Purchase** for a large parcel (828,000 square miles, to be exact) of land that belonged to France—thereby doubling the United States' in land mass. Jefferson also ordered the famed 1804–1806 expedition of Lewis and Clark, in which two white settler colonialists and their crew relied on Sacagawea, a Lemhi Shoshone woman, and her family to steward them across the continent to survey the areas out to the intriguing and potentially conquerable lands near the Pacific Coast. The **Monroe Doctrine**, set down by President James Monroe, added another layer of American influence to both North and South America, claiming that any European invasion of either continent would be considered an act of war on the United States.

## VI. The Founding of Mexico

Before there was a European presence in Mexico, the land was inhabited by Indigenous tribes such as the Aztecs. It was the Aztecs who first interacted with Spanish captains and Catholic missionaries, who began to arrive in the early 1500s. In 1598, the Spanish settler Juan de Oñate embarked, with five hundred soldiers, on a campaign to conquer and colonize lands around the Rio Grande. This border drawing confirmed Spain's settler-colonial project of present-day Mexico, California, Arizona, New Mexico, and Texas.

In the early 1800s, Mexicans waged a war for their independence from Spain and won. On August 24, 1821, Spain signed the Treaty of Córdoba, which gave Mexico its independence and control of the border. At the time of Mexican independence, the northern border of Mexico was drawn above the present-day states of California, Nevada, Wyoming, Utah, Texas, Arizona, and New Mexico, and also included parts of Kansas, Colorado, and Oklahoma.

In the coming years, the newly independent Mexican government was concerned with the number of unauthorized US immigrants entering Mexico. In 1830, Mexico banned US immigration into Coahuila y Tejas—now known as Texas. However, the US immigrants, perhaps motivated by the concept of Manifest Destiny, would not yield their claim to the land. In 1835, another war was waged, this time between white Texas settlers and Mexico. It would result in the independence of Texas, and the bloodshed of many Mexicans in that region. Though Mexico never fully ceded Coahuila y Tejas to the independent Texans, in 1844 Texas was annexed into the United States as a territory. In just twenty-three years, the southern border had been redrawn twice. But the larger battle to draw the border was far from over.

## VII. Two Rivers

Tensions were high between the United States and Mexico when the United States annexed Texas in 1844, and they boiled over when each country claimed ownership over the land between two rivers only 150 miles apart: the Nueces and the Rio Grande. The Nueces River, north of the Rio Grande and much shorter, was the official border of Texas at the time. It also curved to the north, instead of to the east and west like the Rio Grande. President James K. Polk, who was a fervent believer in Manifest Destiny, wanted to extend the US border down to the Rio Grande. His argument was that by following the longer and more substantial southern river, the United States would eventually be able to take Mexico's coastal lands—now known to us as the State of California.

The United States declared war on Mexico in 1846, when soldiers clashed at the Nueces River. The Mexican-American War lasted until September 1847, when the Mexican government surrendered. At the end of the war, the Treaty of Guadalupe Hidalgo was signed between the United States and Mexico on February 2, 1848. The treaty gave over half of Mexico's land mass to the United States, including land that we now know as California and Nevada, as well as parts of Colorado, Arizona, New Mexico, and Wyoming. With the Treaty of Guadalupe Hidalgo, Mexico also gave up all claim to Texas and officially marked the Rio Grande as America's southern border. For this recognition, the United States paid Mexico $15 million. President James K. Polk had taken Manifest Destiny literally. Through bloodshed and force, he had a hand in drawing the border nearly to the degree it is drawn today.

With the signing of the treaty, Indigenous people of the area, whose ancestral lands spanned from central Mexico into what is now the southwestern United States, had to contend with a border drawn through the middle of their lands. This split identity, this morphing of land from being one country's to another's, was not too long ago. It preceded the American Civil War by only thirteen years and World War II by only ninety-one years. At the time of this writing, Mexico has only been independent from Spanish rule for two hundred years.

Today, the borderlands are spoken of as a fixed entity—with the building of walls, the tracking of crossings, patrols, officials, enforcers. The border may convey a sense of permanence, but that is not part of the nature of the land on which it is drawn. According to Carlyn Osborn, a librarian at the Library of Congress, in the years since the Treaty of Guadalupe Hidalgo was signed in 1848, the Rio Grande has changed course several times, as rivers do. This has caused disputes between the United States and Mexico. Issues like flooding, erosion, falling banks, and loss of land are now being monitored by the International Boundary and Water Commission. After all, rivers are known to carve canyons into mountainsides. Who can say what the future holds?

## VIII. Mexican Immigration in the Twentieth Century

For years after the Treaty of Guadalupe Hidalgo was signed, the border between the United States and Mexico operated with an openness embraced by both countries. It was customary for one's workplace and one's home to straddle borders. This was even commemorated in writing within the treaty: "property of every kind, now belonging to Mexicans now established there shall be inviolably respected. The present owners, the heirs of these, and all Mexicans who may hereafter acquire said properties by contract, shall enjoy with respect to its guarantees equally ample as if the same belonged to citizens of the United States."

However, over the next several decades, this idea would be disrespected, and Mexicans found new borders to contend with, including what kind of work they would be able to take part in and what rights they were afforded. This shifting sentiment carried into the early twentieth century, when various presidents would enact welcoming programs to Mexican migrant workers like the Bracero Program, while other presidents enacted Mexican repatriation programs, which modeled early forms of deportation. In the later twentieth century, border crossings would become heavily criminalized, and power was given to local law enforcement in border states. People crossing the borders would undergo drastic measures to make the journey through the desert, risking death or deportation. Ideas and policies about the border shift and change, much like the Rio Grande itself, and those who are impacted most are the people at the center.

As writer Suketu Mehta says, "Before you ask other people to respect the borders of the West, ask yourself if the West has ever respected anybody else's border." In other words, when we think of immigrants as newcomers arriving to *our* lands with intent to live in *our* home, we should take a moment to remember that the Founders believed it was their God-given right to occupy new lands, to call them home. It still informs how our border is drawn. The question is—given the history of how often it has shifted—should we consider that border as fixed, or as something that might change again someday?

## LET'S TALK ABOUT IT

* Historian Roxanne Dunbar-Ortiz says, "People conquered by war and dominated by an imperialist power are not immigrants." What do you think she means by that? Do you agree or disagree, and why?

# CHAPTER 4
## EARLY WAVES OF IMMIGRATION

Because the United States is such a young country, many of the early laws set down during its founding established a precedent that would be followed—consciously or unconsciously—in the crafting and shaping of future laws and ideologies. In order to fully set the stage for twentieth and twenty-first century immigration, we can turn even further back in time to look at another area of immigration history: the first waves of early immigrants, settlers, and refugees from Europe.

It is possible to see patterns in the stories of these people and their arrival that will clearly speak to stories we hear today. Some of those patterns include how the settled

Americans treated anyone newly arrived with animosity, aggression, and disdain. It is clear that many communities who arrived in the United States during its youthful period, as a collection of colonies or as a new nation, had to overcome less-than-welcoming circumstances in order to feel a sense of belonging. Often, that striving for a sense of belonging led to shifts in their own identities. This is the very root of assimilation, which was defined in Chapter 1, and takes on very specific meanings in the stories that we will visit in this chapter.

In its early years, the United States government was already enacting violence on two marginalized groups: Indigenous people and enslaved Africans. The settlers' treatment of these two groups set a precedent: that race would play a factor in how communities of new and unwelcome people were treated in America.

## WHAT'S THAT WORD?

A *marginalized community* is any group of people who are considered peripheral by the majority population. Though the people of these groups have voices, they are typically not heard by the majority. Because of this, marginalized groups and people are often underrepresented.

In this chapter, we will look at different waves of early immigrant communities, namely European settlers, many of whom were ostracized, or shunned, upon their arrival in the United States but whose assimilation arcs relied on proximity to whiteness in order to find their senses of belonging over time. We will also chart the precedent, or prior circumstances or arguments, set in legal battles around these communities' arrivals, which paved the way for the immigration laws and government institutions in existence today.

## WHAT'S THAT WORD?

The National Museum of African American History and Culture defines *whiteness* this way: "Whiteness and white racialized identity refer to the way that white people, their customs, culture, and beliefs operate as the standard by which all other groups of [people] are compared. Whiteness is also at the core of understanding race in America. Whiteness and the normalization of white racial identity throughout America's history have created a culture where nonwhite persons are seen as inferior or abnormal."

Based on the construct of whiteness, someone who identifies as white can move more freely in our country. The unspoken racial caste system (a hierarchy based on race) in America, and its foundations in white supremacist ideologies like slavery and Native American genocide, give power to this construct. New arriving groups could align with the groups in power for their own benefit and inclusion by taking on the ideologies of the group in power. Whether it was based in microaggressions toward less powerful groups, violence motivated by race, or simply adopting unequal precedents set by the group in power, the ability to align and assimilate in America was often based on race.

The communities we will meet in this chapter—the German settlers, the Irish refugees, and the Italian immigrants—all made choices that aligned themselves with whiteness. And we will chart their path from exclusion to inclusion as we also reckon with why many of them chose to take the side of the oppressor rather than the oppressed. At the same time, they shielded themselves from ostracization by leaning into their tight-knit communities, pooling resources, and building their own customs. Many of these communities still exist in some way today, and they mirror ways in which many future immigrant communities will operate once they arrive in America.

Once the United States ratified its Constitution in 1788, the Founders set about to determine how to classify and quantify who counted as "American." Many of the choices that the Founders made around this subject indicate some hard truths. For example, the fact that enslaved Africans and their descendants, Indigenous people, and women were left out of the Constitution speaks volumes about who America really was intended for. When it came to immigration, the 1790 Naturalization Act was the first act quantifying Americanness regarding newcomers. The bill limited citizenship to white immigrants from Western Europe who had resided in the United States for two years and to their children under twenty-one years old. This law, while it would be overruled and rewritten over time, set a damaging precedent of Americanness that is still being undone.

## II. German Settlers

German settlers had been arriving to North America since the 1600s. Some were even part of the earliest settler colonies, like Jamestown and New Amsterdam. Many moved to North America in pursuit of religious freedom, like the early Amish and Mennonite settlers who arrived and began communities in Pennsylvania. Despite their presence in some of the earliest settler colonies, Germans were much maligned by one of the most impactful Founders.

Benjamin Franklin held a prejudice against Germans, and it was reflected in many of his essays and correspondence. By modern-day approximations, he could be called a "child of immigrants." His father, a candlemaker, was born in England (though his mother was born in Massachusetts). Franklin wrote about his worry that the newly settled thirteen colonies would have to deal with the scourge of lower-caste Europeans joining them on their shores. In 1755, Benjamin Franklin published an essay called "Observations Concerning the

Increasing of Mankind, Peopling of Countries, &c." In his essay, Franklin spoke ill of German populations moving to the American colonies, stating,

> And since Detachments of English from Britain sent to America, will have their Places at Home so soon supply'd and increase so largely here; why should the Palatine Boors [Germans] be suffered to swarm into our Settlements, and by herding together establish their Language and Manners to the Exclusion of ours? Why should Pennsylvania, founded by the English, become a Colony of Aliens, who will shortly be so numerous as to Germanize us instead of our Anglifying them, and will never adopt our Language or Customs, any more than they can acquire our Complexion.

Franklin was not the only Founder with a prejudice against the Germans. Thomas Jefferson, a Founder alongside Franklin, shared some views about the Germans. He once wrote, "As to other foreigners it is thought better to discourage their settling together in large masses, wherein, as in our German settlements, they preserve for a long time their own languages, habits, and principles of government."

Franklin counted himself among the English, and so perhaps his prejudice is rooted in tensions between those communities back in Europe. His attitude toward the Germans was a form of prejudice common in the days before Europe was united, before those regions were even thought of as independent nations—the long history of land wars, raids, and pillages, and tensions between rival communities extended over generations. However, Franklin also signed the Declaration of Independence, which contains the line, "We hold these truths to be self-evident, that all men are created equal, that they are endowed by their Creator with certain unalienable Rights." Here in the new thirteen colonies, it was already clear that this oft-quoted cornerstone of American history was untrue. Perhaps Franklin was following prejudicial precedent.

So, did Benjamin Franklin's prejudices inform how America continues to view new arrivals? It's very possible. Recent news articles about the current immigration debate have cited Franklin's injurious writing about Germans as a precedent for immigrant stereotypes. His use of dehumanizing language in his anti-German essay, with words like *swarm* and *herding*, certainly set the standard for using hateful rhetoric in debates around immigrants—a practice still employed today. Franklin wrote a letter to his friend Peter Collinson, a member of the Royal Society in London, describing his wishes for German settlers to assimilate by ensuring they learn the English language, letting their children attend English schools, and tracking or even limiting the number of Germans allowed on ships.

These ideas also sound familiar. Some politicians and pundits today speak of current immigrants in a similar manner, fearing their impact on culture and fearing what impact they will have as part of society. Today, many policies and refugee and asylum restrictions (which we will discuss more in Chapter 8) mirror Franklin's logic. In his letter to Collinson, he stated further that he was "not against the Admission of Germans in general, for they have their Virtues. . . . They are excellent husbandmen and contribute greatly to the improvement of a Country." Even with his prejudices, Franklin did acknowledge that these new arrivals would benefit the new nation.

And with that sentiment, the young nation set about trying to figure out how arrivals would determine into the equation. Once the United States won its war for independence, it began to pass laws that dictated who could be considered American, and when. In 1798, the Alien and Sedition Acts were passed—some of the United States' first laws dealing with immigration and new arrivals. The argument over the laws centered around how long newcomers had to reside in the

United States before they could be eligible for citizenship—the number was increased from five to fourteen years. The laws also gave the president the legal right to forcefully deport immigrants. The connection between Benjamin Franklin's anti-German sentiment and the passage of this law is clear—if newcomers didn't adhere to the *English-bred* version of American customs, language, and ways of life, then they would not be accepted in the new United States. It was assumed that such an assimilation was possible but would take time—fourteen years, to be exact—and only after that would newcomers be able to use their voices at the ballot box.

So how did Germans fare amid all these prejudices? Many turned inward, to their communities, to one another. In Pennsylvania, Amish and Mennonites founded towns where they could practice their religions and maintain customs. In later years, many Germans settled in the Midwest, where they were able to farm familiar crops and maintain traditional harvest celebrations. Others forged communities in the South, where many became enslavers. Thus, some German communities became direct proponents of the culture of white supremacy, a move toward aligning with the people in power, a move toward cementing white supremacy and a solidifying of the period of American slavery. So, sometimes for worse and sometimes for better, communities of German immigrants did assimilate, maintaining some of their culture and identity, while also taking on some of the culture they were joining.

But fights around immigration were just beginning, and by the 1800s, anti-immigrant politicians and thinkers had a new community to target.

### III. Irish Refugees

Today, there are nearly thirty-two million people who claim Irish ancestry living in the United States. There are only five million people living in Ireland! The Irish had a history of dealing with the same colonizer who laid claim to the United States: Great Britain. The British Empire held power over several regions at the far reaches of the world, but one of their longest-run colonies was Ireland, which they had occupied in various ways since 1169. In the mid-1800s, the land was mostly owned and controlled by the British, and the Irish were forced to work as tenant farmers. Because of this, they were forced to export most of the food they grew, leaving many families to starve. One of the only crops that they were allowed to grow and harvest for themselves was a varietal of white potato, another product of imperialism brought over from South America to the British Isles. In 1845, when that white potato varietal was planted in Ireland, the crops caught a disease—a fungus-like organism called *Phytophthora infestans* (or *P. infestans*)—and rotted. The failing crop was disastrous, and as a result, famine overtook Ireland. One million Irish people died in the years of famine that followed. Without food, or adequate power to demand fairer tariffs and ration regulations, many Irish decided to leave their homeland and venture across the ocean to America.

The Irish who settled in the 1840s were part of a mass migration away from the famine and poverty that was afflicting their home country. The Library of Congress states that "census figures show an Irish population of 8.2 million in 1841, 6.6 million a decade later, and only 4.7 million in 1891. It is estimated that as many as 4.5 million Irish arrived in America between 1820 and 1930." The Irish who were fleeing unlivable conditions in Ireland were in fact refugees.

In thinking of the potato famine as a natural disaster, as well as one that was brought about due to colonizers' oppression, the Irish who emigrated from Ireland in this time frame can wear that moniker proudly. These Irish refugees sought life in the United States as a means of survival, and they were willing to face discrimination and a lack of meaningful opportunities in skilled labor in order to put down roots that would aid their families' futures.

The wave of Irish immigration was not without a battle. Anti-immigrant sentiment swelled in the 1830s and 1840s, when Irish and German immigrants continued to make their homes along the eastern seaboard. Descendants of white Protestant settlers were fearful of these newcomers, worried that their jobs would be taken or that their resources would be slimmed. As a divide cemented between these nativists and the new immigrants, the nativists decided to band together in solidarity, publishing anti-immigrant propaganda and pushing anti-immigrant legislation. This new political party refused to answer questions about its operations or beliefs, and so the name the Know-Nothings was born. Though the Know-Nothing Party faded from prominence in the following decades, there is a familiarity to it. Many similar

## WHAT'S THAT WORD?

**Nativism** is an ideology or policy that believes that native-born or established inhabitants of a country are more important than immigrants.

arguments arise about immigrant communities today.

When Irish immigrants arrived, they were met with scorn from the British settlers and their descendants, who carried their old prejudices with them across the sea. In order to deal with the prejudices they felt as newcomers, the Irish did what the Germans did. Many early Irish refugees settled in communities that were predominantly Irish. Irish communities sprouted up in areas with denser populations, like the larger East Coast cities of Boston and New York. There, they formed communities inside neighborhoods and tenements, buildings that were often overcrowded and under resourced.

Anti-Irish sentiment and propaganda rippled through the United States, much of it promoted by the Know-Nothing Party and other nativists. As a tight-knit group, new Irish Americans wanted to keep their families and communities together, but they also yearned for agency and legitimacy. They yearned for power. And in a country that is built upon a framework based in white supremacy, that meant that they leaned into their whiteness, in very specific ways.

In northern cities, new patrols were being created, modeled after slave patrols in the South. Slave patrols were groups of hired men who would enforce laws of slavery by capturing and torturing enslaved people who were attempting to run toward freedom.

## A CLOSER LOOK: NOEL IGNATIEV

**Noel Ignatiev** (1940–2019) was an American historian and thinker who wrote a famous book about whiteness and its hold on society, one that looks exclusively at the plight of early Irish immigrants. That book is called *How the Irish Became White*, and while the book is controversial, it is one of the first books that draws a clear picture of existing racial hierarchies, or caste systems, present in United States history—the same systems and hierarchies that new immigrants are forced to contend with today. While America is thankfully past its era as a nation of enslavers, we still contend with the effects of this foundational identity on our society, our institutions, our government, and our neighbors. Only by looking at this hard history, and our proximity to it, can we hope to move forward with justice.

## IV. Jewish Refugees

Antisemitism, or the hatred and persecution of Jewish

people, is on the rise again in America today. The Anti-Defamation League reported more than two thousand antisemitic incidents in 2020, which is the third-highest year on record. In 2022, a synagogue was held hostage near Fort Worth, Texas, and in recent years Jewish communities have been victims of mass shootings, vandalizations, assaults, and harassment. Books about Jewish history, including books that outline the history of the Holocaust, are being banned in schools in certain states. Antisemitism has had a long history within many cultures, and because of it, Jewish communities have a history of displacement to escape danger and genocide. Jewish refugees have been coming to America to escape persecution for hundreds of years, making new homes in cities and small towns across the United States, and in some cases preceding the arrival of many other European groups to North America.

The earliest Jewish settlers to arrive to North America were Sephardic Jews—the descendants of Jews from Spain and Portugal—who arrived in 1654 from Brazil. Jewish immigrants from central and eastern Europe, also known as Ashkenazi Jews, arrived shortly thereafter, and by 1730, they made up the majority of the Jewish population in

North America. In the 1800s, Jewish refugees arrived from Russia, eastern Europe, and Germany. They settled across America, including in major cities such as Philadelphia, New York, Baltimore, Cincinnati, Albany, Cleveland, Louisville, Minneapolis, St. Louis, New Orleans, and San Francisco.

Many of the Jewish refugees from Russia, Ukraine, and eastern Europe who came to America between 1880 and 1924 were escaping pogroms or other forms of persecution in their homelands. A *pogrom* is the targeted massacre of an ethnic group, or a riot aimed at the destruction of an ethnic group's property. In 1882, the Russian Tsar Alexander III passed a series of antisemitic laws called the May Laws that restricted where Jews could live as well as how and with whom they could conduct business. Elsewhere, Jewish businesses were vandalized, and property was destroyed. Many, fearing for their lives and their safety, arranged to leave their homelands to find a peaceful existence elsewhere. And, as is the story of so many immigrants, they set their hopes on a future in the United States.

Just before the opening of Ellis Island in 1892, New York Harbor's brand-new immigration processing center, President Benjamin Harrison ordered a commission to study the increased emigration from Europe. Colonel John B. Weber traveled to Russia as part of the commission, and he determined that Jews were immigrating to America because of religious and ethnic persecution. Jewish immigrants made up a large portion of immigrants who came through Ellis Island, which we will cover in the next chapter. Many members of the growing Jewish community in New York City created aid societies like the Hebrew Immigrant Aid Society and the United Hebrew Charities of New York. These organizations helped new Jewish immigrants with translation and to find jobs and places to live. It was an early example of community care and mutual aid that allowed many Jewish immigrants to enrich and deepen their newfound community in America. In the late 1800s through the early 1900s, many Jews settled alongside other New York City newcomers in tenement housing on the Lower East Side. A tenement is a building, typically with apartments inhabited by multiple people, shared entryways, and often communal bathrooms. Men, women, and even children took labor-intensive jobs in the garment district. Many of these small apartment buildings still stand, and you can wind up and down these narrow side streets nestled between New York City's historic Chinatown,

Little Italy, and East Village neighborhoods.

In March of every year, if you take a walk down these streets, you might come upon the chalk-written names of women and their ages on the sidewalk in front of one of these buildings. These names are in memory of the Triangle Shirtwaist Factory Fire in 1911, a tragic blaze in a Lower Manhattan garment factory that killed 146 workers, most of them young Jewish women, and many of them recent immigrants. In the wake of the tragedy, survivors and women activists protested, calling for rights and safety in the workplace. Because of the efforts of these Jewish immigrants, the New York State Committee on Safety was established, and several subsequent labor laws were passed, to the benefit of all American workers.

In 1939, a passenger ship filled with Jewish refugees escaping Nazi Germany sailed to Cuba, where only 28 of its 937 passengers were granted visas. The remaining Jewish refugees were refused entry to Florida and Canada and were forced to return on the ship back to Europe, where one third would perish in the Holocaust. Because of existing prejudices around this immigrant group, and largely because of rampant antisemitism, these refugees were, in the words of one survivor, "abandoned by the world." This tragedy was a major factor in the establishment of many modern-day refugee-aid organizations, in an attempt to make sure that prejudices against religion never again determine the fate of a refugee.

As with the other oppressed or marginalized groups in this chapter, Jewish people straddle an ever-changing idea of whiteness. Perhaps Jewish people in the present day may be white-presenting, yet it is important to recognize that they are also considered a race. Historically, Jewish people have been persecuted as a race. As Daniella Greenbaum writes for the *Washington Post*, "[Antisemitism] is older, and different—and in some ways, more deeply embedded—than the forms of racism Americans are used to recognizing." It is important to remember that while our notions of whiteness as a culture may have changed, we cannot forget the specific details of the traumatic histories that these communities have endured in the name of whiteness.

Throughout American history, Jewish activists have been on the front lines of promoting change in our country. In 1924, the prohibitive Immigration Act was passed, which restricted immigration based on national origins. This law had a hand in preventing many Holocaust refugees from fleeing Europe in the 1930s. However, Jewish activists were vocal opponents of the law, and they helped to overturn it with the passage of the Immigration and Nationality Act of 1965.

Jewish communities are part of every geographic region of the United States. Perhaps their ancestors arrived two hundred years ago—or maybe they are recent immigrants. Either way, knowing more about the history of Jewish refugees in America, and the ways that they have been persecuted at home and abroad, will allow us to eradicate the long cycle of antisemitism that has followed them here. It will also allow us to celebrate the impact of Jewish Americans on our culture, our laws, and our freedoms.

## V. Italian Immigrants

In the year 1870, there were only twenty-five thousand Italian immigrants estimated to be living in the United States. In the next decade, the number would jump exponentially. Italians, especially from the areas of Sardinia and Sicily, began to emigrate to the United States for similar reasons as the Irish did. Though famine was not widespread, it was acute, as was poverty. Italy was newly formed as a nation in 1861, and several different regions with varying customs and dialects were now unified as one country. However, unresolved conflicts between regions and a lack of resources caused an uptick in violence.

From 1880 to 1924, over four million Italians arrived from Italy to the United States. Many passages were conducted through Ellis Island, which opened in 1892 and became the major port of call for newcomers.

Today, Italian Americans are one of the largest ethnic groups in the United States. There are large, thriving Italian communities in several major cities across America, including New York City, New Orleans, Chicago, and the Bay Area in California. Many of those communities started small, with new arrivals at the turn of the twentieth century living in cramped tenement housing, pooling resources, and trying to find one another jobs.

Italians wanted to work, and many wanted to take part in the industrial revolution, but they had a hard time finding employment. This was because of prejudice. Historian Roxanne Dunbar-Ortiz writes, "Italian migrants were met with endless insults in newspapers and magazines, which described them as . . . criminally inclined." Discrimination followed Italians of all ages through their early American experience: Children were often denied enrollment in school, while women were denied entry to public places like churches. According to Dunbar-Ortiz, the US House Committee on Immigration even had a debate in 1912 about whether Italians could be considered "full-blooded Caucasians."

These loud proclamations, based on false and racist ideologies of presumed worth, made it hard for Italians to assimilate. It wasn't until a federal holiday honoring Christopher Columbus, an Italian, was announced that Italians started to be accepted.

The Italian claiming of Columbus did eventually aid in the assimilation of Italians into the white, Anglo-Saxon, Protestant American society. In 1934, Columbus Day was made a federal holiday, and soon Italians were seeing gains in their employment and securing futures that had been denied to them only decades prior.

## A CLOSER LOOK: THE LEGACY OF CHRISTOPHER COLUMBUS

Christopher Columbus, whose name has been Anglicized from his given Italian name, Cristoforo Colombo, was an explorer whose legacy is often seen through the faulty lens of hard history. His arrival in 1492 to the Western Hemisphere has been mythologized into a role alongside the American Founders. The truth is, Columbus never stepped foot on continental North America. His lionization as an American hero at the turn of the twentieth century was perpetuated by Italian Americans, who began to refer to Columbus as "the first immigrant" to America. This attachment to Columbus, says historian Danielle Battisti, gave Italian Americans a "formative role in the nation-building narrative." By perpetuating the false myth that Columbus "discovered" America, Italians were also participating in not only the erasure of true Indigenous history but the glorification of Columbus's ties to a painful, violent, and genocidal history. Many Indigenous leaders have spoken out about the pain of Columbus's perceived heroism, and in 2021, President Biden proclaimed that Columbus Day would also be named Indigenous Peoples' Day.

The German, Irish, Italian, and Jewish immigrant communities of our nation's history all mirror a trend that continues with American immigrant populations today. In order to assimilate, communities of immigrants rely on one another for help with jobs, naturalization and citizenship, and childcare. They often pool resources, start businesses together, and move to similar cities and towns, where they can speak their native languages and rely on one another for emotional support. And, in the struggle to assimilate, they may make choices that continue to perpetuate some of the ugliest cycles in our country's history.

In learning more about these immigrants, one thing to take away and reflect on is how each of these groups was treated upon their arrival. American citizens were not welcoming to these new groups, and they made it known with insults, discrimination, and violence. When we take a look back, sometimes we learn what not to do. What can be accomplished when newcomers' humanity is acknowledged? Might the cycle of assimilation, and its impact on other marginalized communities, be broken? Might it stop the cycle of marginalized groups oppressing one another, in the name of power and racist ideology?

The Italian American writer Gay Talese once said, "And so you know the difficulty in becoming an American. It isn't a sudden process. You get over it. But you don't ever quite get over it. You carry it with you. That's the great—and not so great—aspect of being or trying to be an assimilated American." How can we help shoulder the burden of our new neighbors, in the name of building a better and more equal country for all?

## LET'S TALK ABOUT IT

*In thinking of early Irish immigrants as refugees, what parallels might you draw between their reasons for arriving to America and refugees' reasons today?

*Each of these early groups were discriminated against in different ways upon their arrival to the United States. What do you think that discrimination made them feel? How might it have impacted them and their children?

# CHAPTER 5
## THE STATUE OF LIBERTY,
## THE GOLDEN DOOR

I recently visited the Statue of Liberty. As I looked up, I could not help but be in awe of her. I have lived in New York City for seventeen years, and I had never visited the statue before. Even from the shores of Manhattan, from the vantage point of the fenced-off park that looks out onto New York Harbor, I have always thought that the Statue of Liberty looked smaller than I expected. But up close, she is marvelous to behold. Lady Liberty, as the statue is affectionately known, was meant to be a paragon—the perfect example—of liberty and freedom for our country. Did those newcomers know what it really stood for?

Clarence Haynes, in his book in the True History series called *The Legacy of Jim Crow*, discusses the Statue of Liberty's origins. It was a gift from the French, sculpted by an artist named Frédéric-Auguste Bartholdi, who may have originally designed Lady Liberty to be holding up a broken shackle in honor of the abolition of slavery. Of course, when we look at pictures of the Statue of Liberty (or get on that windy ferry to visit her for ourselves), we notice that she is not holding broken chains but a tablet. The tablet she holds is dated July 4, 1776, when Congress approved the Declaration of Independence. As I walked the grounds, I tried to put myself in the shoes of a passenger upon a ship, finally seeing land after days of seeing only sea, finally reaching the end of a long journey.

On the grounds of the Statue of Liberty is a plaque inscribed with the famous poem by Emma Lazarus called "The New Colossus." The poem reads:

*Not like the brazen giant of Greek fame,*
*With conquering limbs astride from land to land;*
*Here at our sea-washed, sunset gates shall stand*
*A mighty woman with a torch, whose flame*
*Is the imprisoned lightning, and her name*
*Mother of Exiles. From her beacon-hand*

*Glows world-wide welcome; her mild eyes command*
*The air-bridged harbor that twin cities frame.*
*"Keep, ancient lands, your storied pomp!" cries she*
*With silent lips. "Give me your tired, your poor,*
*Your huddled masses yearning to breathe free,*
*The wretched refuse of your teeming shore.*
*Send these, the homeless, tempest-tost to me,*
*I lift my lamp beside the golden door!*

Lazarus wrote the poem in 1883, and today it is synonymous with the plight of the immigrant. I always assumed that the poem was written as a response to the art, grace, and symbolism of the Statue of Liberty, or perhaps a response to that same scene described on my ferry—an account of ships arriving at Ellis Island, their passengers inspired, hopeful, and cheering at the sight of Lady Liberty.

The poem is often quoted in response to immigration policy as it is enacted, especially the line "Give me your tired, your poor, / Your huddled masses yearning to breathe free." It seemingly alludes to Lady Liberty's comforting presence to those immigrants being welcomed to our shores. In fact, Lazarus wrote the poem before the statue was even erected. It was written to raise money at an auction to fundraise for the statue's pedestal. The statue was not even dedicated until the year 1886. And, in fact, Ellis Island was not operational until 1892, so my theory about Lazarus describing boats arriving there was wrong as well!

Another interesting fact is the timing. In 1882, the year before Lazarus wrote a poem extolling the virtues and symbols of a welcoming nation, the US Congress passed the Chinese Exclusion Act, one of the most severe, ostracizing, and racist immigration laws to ever be passed in America. (The Chinese Exclusion Act, and other significant history of the Asian American immigrant experience, will be discussed further in Chapter 6.)

Since she was installed and dedicated in New York in 1886, the Statue of Liberty has become an American symbol of freedom and opportunity. And sometimes, she has been taken up as an American symbol for hate. For instance, anti-immigration editorial cartoons from the late nineteenth century depict Lady Liberty as a gatekeeper, a racist joke, or an object susceptible to stereotypical immigrant-rooted fears like disease and crime.

The story of her change in design seems, in many ways, a metaphor or symbol for our country. One not only of hope but of false promises, of covered-up tragedies, of complicity and commerce. I took one last picture as I hoped that we can continue to work against the wrongs of our origins. And I made my way back to the ferry for my next stop.

## II. Ellis Island

Ellis Island was once a port of first call for people who hoped to migrate to the United States. Located at the mouth of the Hudson River, nestled between New York, New Jersey, and the Statue of Liberty, it is now home to the National Immigration Museum. Ellis Island is made up of three conjoined land masses: Island 1, Island 2, and Island 3. From 1892 until 1954, passenger ships would dock in New York Harbor and send ferries of their passengers to be processed at Ellis Island before they could continue on to their final destination on the United States' mainland. Today, the museum at Ellis Island allows attendees to roam the halls of the first landing point for hopeful new Americans, to learn more about the process of their arrivals, and to research where migration intersects with their own genealogic histories.

To get to Ellis Island from Manhattan, you have to travel to the southernmost tip of the island of Manhattan. Then, a ferry from Castle Clinton in Battery Park will stop first at the

Statue of Liberty before continuing on to Ellis Island. On the ferry, a voice on the loudspeakers will explain how waves of cheering would erupt from the boats after their long voyage led to them seeing the Statue of Liberty poke out from the horizon. In our nostalgic look back at those immigrants—perhaps among them our grandparents, great-grandparents, or ancestral lineages—we attempt to seek out the hope and the potential in those origin stories.

But what was the process of arriving to the United States really like in the time of Ellis Island? How does it differ or align with the practices utilized in immigration processing today? And for those who made it through all the checkpoints and barriers, what did their futures hold in store?

On my first trip to Ellis Island, I walked up a set of stairs with my audio guide in hand, unknowingly walking up a very consequential staircase. When I arrived at the second-floor landing, I found myself in the Registry Room, a large, cavernous space replete with columns, archways, and two large American flags. I listened to my audio guide, whose narrator told me about the stairway I had just walked up: Immigrants walking up that stairway were already unwittingly being monitored by doctors, who were looking for a litany of symptoms ranging from small to large, in order to classify and quantify the viability of the newcomer in question. I learned it would take doctors only six seconds to determine who was well enough to make it through the inspection and who would need to be detained.

In the center of the Registry Room are rows of pews where new arrivals sat, awaiting their interviews with the officials whose podiums line the other end of the room. Behind the podiums, another series of stairways, each leading to a different fate. They are called the Stairs of Separation. One, to the left, leads to the railway ticket room—a sure sign that their documentation was processed and their arrival to the United States was approved. Another, to the right, was for approved immigrants who wanted to exchange currency before embarking on their next journey. The middle stairway was the least favored: Being sent down that stairway was a sign that you might be too sick, too old, or too "unfit" to stay in America. You were either sent back to your ship or to the onsite hospital for further evaluation.

For most immigrants coming through Ellis Island, the whole process would take between three and seven hours. When immigrants were detained at Ellis Island, several factors determined how long they would stay and whether they would make it through the "golden door" at all. If the doctors marked a person's coat with a symbol for a certain disease, that immigrant may have to be detained until they were determined to be no longer contagious. Women who were deemed too far along in their pregnancy had to stay until their babies were born. Some had to spend weeks, or even months, quarantined in the detention center, with uncomfortable cots for beds and little to no privacy.

My experience of the museum exhibits about detainees left me feeling a sense of uncertainty. The interviewees, recounting their experiences, did not necessarily view those experiences with a positive lens. The barracks in which they slept, the close confines, and the lack of communication they may have felt, all most likely contributed to this. However, the museum's portrayal of the detainee experience is written and framed with a positive spin. For example, the audio guide narrator references the positive accounts and memories of the food given to the detainees. I imagined that framings such as this were designed for a child's sensitive perception of the realities of the hardship endured by those who made passage to the United States. This made me want to know what information I would glean about the experience from another perspective than that of the institution.

Ellis Island's history as a detention center did not stop with immigrants. During World War II, at a time when few to no immigrants were being processed into the United States, the island served as a wartime jail for enemies of the state. It also ramped up deportation efforts during that time.

From 1892 until 1954, Ellis Island ushered in over twelve million immigrants to the United States, most of them before 1924, when a strict immigration quota law was passed. Approximately 20 percent of those immigrants were detained temporarily on the island. 250,000 were denied entry and deported. 3,500 people died on Ellis Island, presumably during a period of detainment. And, surprisingly, 350 babies were born there in the hospital maternity ward.

## III. The Big Book of Names

When I arrived, I had assumed I would be riffling for my family's information in a giant book of names. Perhaps some registry akin to a guest book that housed the arrival information of every steward to this land. Something we might see an official use in conversations with a new immigrant, in movies like *An American Tail*. But I was wrong. When I arrived at the Passenger Search database, I found it to look more like a research center in a high-school library. Kiosks with computers are available for folks whose ancestors passed through this processing center, and for a fee, you can search the database for ancestral information, including the year of their arrival, the ship they were on, and a look at the ship's manifest.

When I asked a museum security guard about the existence of the book of names I had in my mind, she laughed and said that it did not exist, but that it was a common question. She went on to tell me that the existence of any record of people who arrived at Ellis Island was documented inside each ship's manifest, or crew and passenger log, and that manifest was then passed to the guards at Ellis Island to use for processing. I also found out a piece of crucial information that completely shocked me.

## IV. An Old Legend

It's a legend passed down from immigrant to child and eventually to descendant: "Our name was changed at Ellis Island." The story goes that last names were often Anglicized at Ellis Island by the agents who were working in the Registry Room. At Ellis Island, I found out that this legend is not true. Often, immigrants would elect to have their names changed when arriving to America—an act of assimilation, or perhaps a new start in a new land. But the officials would work solely with the names on the passenger-ship manifests. They never had to write names down, only call them out. Were an immigrant to want to change their name, they would have had to change it on the ship, before its arrival at Ellis Island.

The immigration process—both then and now—is filled with institutional barriers that for many can seem too high to climb. In both instances, then and now, we have folks, striving for a better life, who are subject to dehumanizing and reductive practices of quantification. In both instances, we have people arriving to a country claiming to be founded on equality and liberty while in reality serving many opposing principles. In both instances, newcomers are subject to supremacy of language; lost translations; needing to assimilate, to be smart, to be healthy; and being held to standards higher than many existing citizens are held to.

The museum holds a more comprehensive look at the immigration history of America—it includes exhibits on immigration today, the path to citizenship, the struggles of the immigrant. Other exhibits also focus on what it means to leave one's homeland and early encounters between settler colonialists and Indigenous tribes. Today, it seems, the museum at Ellis Island is still attempting to examine its role as part of a larger history.

## A CLOSER LOOK: MY GRANDFATHER'S IMMIGRATION STORY

My grandfather, Rolf Backhaus, was the son of German immigrants whose own parents immigrated through Ellis Island in 1926. When it came time for them to travel to America, they left four-year-old Rolf in Germany in the care of his grandmother. By the time Rolf turned ten, Adolf Hitler had already turned Germany into a police state, during which time "nobody could listen to foreign broadcasts and opponents of the regime ended up in concentration camps." Rolf longed to escape Germany and join his family in the United States, but it wasn't until after World War II that he had a chance. In an essay he wrote in 1986, he describes his memory of his arrival to America:

"On December 19, 1949, our ship, the SS *Washington*, made her way from *Ambrose* Lightship up into New York

Harbor past that great lady, the Statue of Liberty. . . . The passengers were crowding the railings, trying to catch a glimpse of this great symbol of freedom. Well, we had made it to America! . . . I had mixed emotions as we passed Ellis Island, a place my parents had passed through in 1926 on their arrival in the USA. Thank God, we were spared that experience. . . .

As our ship steamed up the Hudson on that Monday morning of December 19, I was thinking of all that new bureaucracy awaiting us in this new land. But what a surprise!

We landed at the United States Lines pier. After a very brief check through US Customs, we joined the waiting people behind the barrier. We were in the land of the free. Nobody told us where to go or what to do. It was scary at first, but we had finally received the first true taste of freedom!

More than thirty-one years ago, my wife and I took the oath of allegiance. We became US citizens on May 31, 1955.

I will never receive the Liberty Medal . . . but I am just as proud to be an American as any one of them, and I thank the good Lord for having granted me the opportunity to experience true freedom in this wonderful country."

## V. A Final Farewell to Lady Liberty

My footsteps patted quietly in the empty hallways; the other museum attendees walked in silence and reverence. It is a different energy than it held at its peak of operation, when thousands of new immigrants would be processed every day—the sounds of several languages pinging and echoing in the registry room, the shuffling of feet and the dragging of luggage, the comforting of tired and fearful children, the tamping down of nerves and worry. The culmination of one journey, the beginning of something new—a bridge to a next chapter that cannot be seen, from this beautiful, terrifying building on an island that straddles past and future.

The museum gleamed, its history washed clean for those who visited it that day. I took one last look before I dashed out to catch my ferry back to Manhattan. What does it mean to walk around somewhere newly polished, knowing that the ancestry of so many walked these halls, unsure of their fates and their futures? What bravery did it take for those tired and weary to be subject to several dehumanizing tests, snap judgments, and criticisms, those long waits, after experiencing trauma, hardship, and consequence in their homelands? For those who were not able-bodied, able-minded, those without money or resources—how much harder it must have been for them to land in America and find solid ground.

**LET'S TALK ABOUT IT**

* Do you think the museum tries to make the immigrant experience sound better than it was for so many of the people coming through Ellis Island? Explain.

# CHAPTER 6
## ASIAN IMMIGRATION AND
## THE CIVIL RIGHTS MOVEMENT

We have John Lewis to thank.

On March 7, 1965, during a national reckoning with systemic racism and inequality, a group of voting rights and civil rights activists engaged in a peaceful march from Selma to Montgomery in Alabama. The march that day was made famous when, on the Edmund Pettus Bridge, the peaceful demonstrators were attacked and brutally beaten by state troopers. The day came to be known as "Bloody Sunday," and became a moment of public awakening to the fight for civil rights for Black Americans. It is a day when America saw injustice, racism, and hate and remembered its conscience.

John Lewis, a young Black civil rights activist who was already famous for his March on Washington speech in 1963, was present that day. State troopers hit him first, and he was beaten so badly that his skull was cracked. A photographer took a photo of the attack, and it was shown on national news. The footage from Bloody Sunday changed the conversation about civil rights, and Americans rallied behind the fight for equality. Lewis continued to work to solidify change and eventually became a prominent figure in politics, from his work in grassroots movements to serving as a United States congressman.

When Lewis passed away in 2020 from cancer, many Asian Americans mourned Lewis's role in their own lives and histories. His work in the civil rights movement, and the stand he and his fellow demonstrators took on Bloody Sunday, would pave the way not only for the passage of the Civil Rights Act of 1964 but also for one of the most impactful and expansive pieces of legislation for Asian American immigrants. The year after the Civil Rights Act was passed, Congress passed the Immigration and Nationality Act of 1965, which widened the road for Asian American immigration to the United States after a century of exclusion, quotas, discrimination, internment, and ostracization.

## II. Who We Are: Asian Americans

The phrase "Asian American" is a solidarity term coined in 1968 by students at the University of California, Berkeley, who were inspired by the Black Power movement, a social movement that began in the 1960s to advocate for Black American rights. The phrase is used to refer to people who have lineages in East Asia, South Asia, West Asia, and Southeast Asia, as well as Pacific Island countries. The Asian continent is a region that holds forty-nine countries, encompasses more than seventeen million square miles, and boasts a population of more than 4.7 billion people today. By no means can we feasibly look at such a massive area of the world and its many peoples as a monolith. While the term seems to insufficiently capture the myriad identities it represents, there is a root to its connectivity that stems from the way immigrants from Asia were treated from the earliest waves to the present day. We will use the term *Asian American* as well as the term *AAPI* (Asian American and Pacific Islander) to refer to the larger population and historical arc, while also zooming in on some particular stories, communities, and individuals whose stories shaped this history.

## III. The Transcontinental Railroad

Asians have been in America for hundreds of years, and they also played a prominent role in building the framework of the newly expanded United States. The transcontinental railroad was one of the last Manifest Destiny projects, linking the East Coast to the West Coast by rail. The project would take many years to complete, and after an unsuccessful hunt for white workers, the Central Pacific Railroad decided to hire Chinese workers. In January 1864, twenty-one Chinese laborers began to build the railroad line. The demand for labor continued to increase, and the work was so dangerous that not many white workers dared to take it on. But Chinese immigrants, many of whom had been unable to find jobs in the port city of San Francisco, were eager to work and took the jobs. By 1867, Chinese immigrants made up 90 percent of the Central Pacific Railroad workforce.

The work was brutal, backbreaking, and deadly. Cathy Park Hong, a Korean American writer and poet, notes that three Chinese rail workers died for every two miles of track laid. Overall, hundreds of Chinese rail workers died from explosions, accidents, and disease. The workers were also discriminated against, receiving lower pay than their white counterparts. After six years of construction, rail lines from the East met the rail lines from the West in Utah and the transcontinental railroad was complete. On May 10, 1869, a ceremony was held where one of the rail bosses joined the rails with a golden spike. When a photograph was taken of the event, the Chinese workers were excluded from it. In the late 1860s, white nativists in San Francisco waged a propaganda campaign against Chinese immigrants, many of whom arrived in the United States to work on the transcontinental railroad, which led to the eventual passage of the Chinese Exclusion Act.

## IV. The Chinese Exclusion Act

In the aftermath of the building of the transcontinental railroad, anti-immigrant sentiment would increase toward the Chinese. Many of the immigrants wanted to naturalize and become citizens, but they faced opposition from their neighbors, cities, and even political parties who ran on an anti-immigrant ticket, or platform. In California, a law was temporarily passed that suspended Chinese citizens' voting rights. It was deemed unconstitutional, and the law was repealed, but only a few years later, on May 6, 1882, the Chinese Exclusion Act was passed. It was the first federal immigration law, and it was one that did not welcome newcomers—it actively kept them out.

The Chinese Exclusion Act ruled that virtually all Chinese immigration would be suspended for a ten-year period. In 1902, the law was renewed indefinitely. The law also banned Chinese citizenship outright. The law was broken frequently, but that was because it was a new precedent—laws and rules about immigration had never behaved this way before. Prior to this law, the United States' immigration laws were more broadly stated, with few specific limits and quotas, so entry to the country was more accessible. In the early waves of immigration, communities of immigrants surely had their struggles. But they were allowed to arrive here. That exact thing—permission—was never on the table for new immigrants. Now that a ban was in place, it would pave the way for similar exclusionary laws, and the implementation of quotas, throughout the twentieth century.

## V. Quotas, Bans, and Internments

Several laws in the next few decades would follow the Chinese Exclusion Act, perpetuating its principles and continuing to build out a confusing barrier to all Asians. In 1917, a new law prevented immigration from anywhere in the "Asiatic Barred Zone." Then, Congress passed the Immigration Act of 1924, which set quotas for immigration based on national origin and prevented entry for any person ineligible for eventual citizenship. The law favored European immigrants over immigrants from anywhere else in the world. Because of precedent set in the 1790 Naturalization Act—and a similar one passed in 1870—Asians were now excluded from entering the country. The Immigration Act of 1924 angered the nation of Japan, whose people were still allowed entry to the United States up until its passing.

These laws did not help public sentiment toward Asians. Racist violence was constant in these times, built on stereotypes that were distributed in speeches, news articles, and political cartoons. These stereotypes even fueled hatred between US citizens and continued to influence laws that would be passed, restricting Asians' constitutional rights. During World War II, Japanese American citizens would be sent to labor camps and stripped of their jobs, material possessions, wealth, and dignity. Asians across the United States lived in fear of mob violence or deportation. The Chinese Exclusion Act was finally repealed in 1943 when Congress passed the Magnuson Act, allowing Chinese Americans and their families to finally apply for citizenship.

By the time the Immigration and Nationality Act was passed in 1965, many tight-knit Asian American communities were already flourishing. With the passage of the new law, quotas based on race and ethnicity were abolished, and the golden doors opened the widest they ever have for AAPI newcomers, with more visas available than ever before. It not only offered opportunities for Asians to immigrate to the United States but also for Africans and Latin Americans as well. Since the law's passage, it is estimated that fifty-nine million immigrants have made their way to the United States. Perhaps the first real sign of America's promise.

## VI. My (Other) Grandfather's Story

My maternal grandparents both passed away the year before I was born, so I never met them. With their passing, my family lost many of the details of the unique immigrant story that saw my grandparents leave Punjab and settle in California over thirty years between 1917 and 1947, as well as the story of their founding role in a community that now boasts one of the single largest concentrations of Sikh diasporic populations in the entire world.

What I did not realize, until more recently, is how tied their story is to the legislation passed by the United States government that made it possible for them to arrive here. And how many barricades, hurdles, and exclusionary laws made it nearly impossible for them to embark on the journey at all.

Yuba City, California, is now home to the annual Sikh Parade, which calls thousands of attendees to Sutter County farm country every November. The parade and festival celebrate the rich history of Sikh immigrants who have been settling in California since the late 1800s. The sons of Didar Singh Bains, one of the area's founding Sikh immigrant farmers, were interviewed by W. Kamau Bell for his documentary show *United Shades of America*. Bains's sons were to speak of their father's arrival in California by boat in the early 1900s, where he was able to establish Bains Family Farms, one of the nation's premier purveyors of peaches, almonds, and prunes. The Bains family's story is very similar to my own family's. We have surmised that Didar Singh Bains and my grandfather, Swarn Singh Takher, were on boats that arrived in California around the same time in 1917.

In 1947, after years working as a farm laborer and eventually saving enough money to buy his own land, my grandfather was able to marry a young woman named Swarn Kaur Bassi (yes, my grandparents had the same first name) and bring her to live with him in the United States. The family moved around the Northern California delta until finally landing in Yuba City. In the mid-1960s, my grandmother's extended family began to join her in the United States, including her younger brother, her sister's children, and her cousins. Takhar Farms is proudly operated by both my uncle and my cousins, and recently on a family trip, we talked of trying to piece together what we know of my grandfather's story.

While doing research for this book, I stumbled upon the revelation that many of the historic dates of immigration laws passed in the twentieth century coincided with my family's immigration narrative. My grandfather's arrival in 1917 was accomplished with some secrecy—it was the same year the United States banned entry from anyone from the "Asiatic Barred Zone." Because of laws that outlawed his ability to either marry outside of his race or bring a wife from Asia with him, he was unable to marry until the British-facilitated partition of India and Pakistan in 1947 caused civil unrest. In response, the United States created accommodations for a small number of refugees, which is how my grandmother arrived. And finally, with the passage of the Immigration and Nationality Act of 1965, previous bans and restrictive quotas on immigration from Asia were lifted, which is when the rest of my grandmother's family were able to join her here.

It is in stories like these—family stories, passed down with lost detail—that we children and grandchildren of immigrants begin to piece together the past. No longer does it become a set of laws, or a series of events on a timeline, but moments of real consequence for people who would have loved us, if only we walked the earth at the same time.

## VII. Asian Americans Today

In the 2020 census, the Asian American population was tallied to twenty-four million, or 7.2 percent of the country's population. They are Korean, Bangladeshi, Thai, Pakistani, Cambodian, Japanese, Vietnamese, Filipino, Hmong, Indian, Laotian. They are first generation, second generation—some are even fifth and sixth generation. They are part of tight-knit communities, where they can speak their languages and practice their customs, and they are our neighbors, our fellow citizens, our friends and loved ones and family. They are myriad, and their stories cannot all be told in this space. But it is important to honor these people, and their immigrant histories—to look at the centuries of sacrifice, of exclusion, and begin to recognize that these stories belong alongside the foundational stories of our nation. That America, at its best, is the sum of the communities it holds.

In 2018, John Lewis, then a member of Congress, was speaking at an immigration rally in Atlanta. More than six hundred rallies were being held across the country that day in support of "Families Belong Together," a movement that opposed family-separation laws being enacted at the United States–Mexico border. Lewis, who was a participant in nonviolent activism until his death, spoke his opinions on the immigrant: "We are one people . . . one family, we all live in the same house. . . . It doesn't matter if you are black or white, Asian American or Native American. . . . There is no such thing as an illegal human being. We are all humans."

# CHAPTER 7
## MOVING FORWARD FROM "GOING BACK"

In 2019, the phrase "go back to your country" made headlines after being invoked by President Trump. In an effort to describe four congresspeople in the House of Representatives who were of an opposing political party, all of whom were women of color, he asked why the congresspeople don't "go back and help fix the totally broken and crime infested places from which they came." Three of the four congresspeople were in fact born in the United States, and the fourth is a United States citizen. Though one might presume that Trump was unaware of the birthplace of these congresspeople, there can be no doubt that this sentiment is often weaponized against people of the global majority whose ancestors or immediate family members immigrated to the United States at some point in their history.

"Go back to your country" is a racially discriminatory phrase that is directed at someone who purportedly is unwelcome in America and therefore does not belong here. The phrase has been documented as being uttered during instances of hate-based violence and racially motivated crime. Sometimes, the people who are told to "go back to their country" are US citizens, so the order to "go back" is meaningless. They are right where they should be: here on American soil. Of course, regardless of one's citizenship status, the phrase is unnecessary; its only purpose is to discriminate.

Jennifer Wingard, a scholar at the University of Houston, describes the phrase as a palimpsest, or a piece of text that has been rewritten or overwritten yet still carries several old meanings. She states, "You know, 'go back where you came from' is the same as 'go back to your own country' is the same as 'you are not allowed here' is the same as 'no immigrants allowed.' Yet it carries all of this historical shorthand with it."

When we remember the notion that our nation was

founded by immigrants and descendants of immigrants, that settler colonialism is a part of this nation's origin, we must consider the implications of the phrase through the long lens of our country's immigration history. For one group of immigrants to be able to assimilate into the nation's population with ease, while another has a harder time based on their country of origin or ethnicity, is an imbalance that can be referred to as the stereotype of the "perpetual foreigner." This is someone who is considered to always be an outsider when it comes to the culture, practices, and ideologies of North American culture and identity. This stereotype, which feeds into larger notions of nativism and white supremacy, jumps to the conclusion that no matter how many generations a person's family has been in the United States, they will somehow seem foreign. This misdirected ideology affects many members of the AAPI community, even though we've learned in the last chapter that Asians were arriving to North America in the nineteenth century.

So what fuels these ideas about who can or cannot assimilate after immigration? Though the accounts of anti-immigrant statements like "Go back to . . ." have been documented in recent news, the long history of this phrase and its sentiment can be linked to some of the earliest anti-immigration legislation passed in our country.

## II. Going Back through the Ages

The wording might be a little different each time, but the motivation remains the same in examples of anti-immigration sentiment through the ages. Wingard traces back to 1798, when Congress passed a series of laws that would make the path to citizenship harder for new immigrants. This included the Alien and Sedition Acts, which laid down new laws for deporting foreigners and made it more difficult for new immigrants to vote. The debate in Congress centered around which of the two political parties at that time, the Democratic-Republicans and the Federalists, new immigrants would vote for (a similar tactic informs immigration debates in the present day). This seemed to affect the debate around the creation of the Alien and Sedition Acts, as one Federalist member of Congress stated that there was no reason to "invite hordes of Wild Irishmen, nor the turbulent and disorderly of all the world, to come here with a basic view to distract our tranquillity [sic]." The passing of the Alien and Sedition Acts was motivated by politics but also by discrimination toward a group of non-English immigrants. Wingard states, "Every wave of immigration that gets in sees the next wave as the threat. That is the wave that is now going to take the jobs, that is now going to take things away. The latest flow in is always the one that seems the most threatening." The United States continued to pass legislation rooted in discrimination and anti-immigrant sentiment in future years, and it affected the safety and well-being of those populations.

And in more recent history, hate crimes and discrimination against Middle Eastern and South Asian populations, specifically Muslim Americans or those perceived to be Muslim, rose in the United States after the September 11 attacks in 2001—the effects of which are felt in those communities to this day. This hostile public sentiment paved the way for the most recent Muslim travel ban, which was put into law by executive order in 2017.

## III. The Story of Balbir Singh Sodhi

Mesa, Arizona (my birthplace), was also home to a man named Balbir Singh Sodhi. Sodhi was a Sikh Punjabi immigrant (like my grandfather), and he made his way to the United States with his six brothers, each arriving with hope for a brighter future. Sodhi owned a gas station in Mesa, and he developed a loving rapport with his customers, offering candy to children and telling customers who could not afford their gas to pay him the next day. On September 15, 2001, a Saturday, he was planting a garden out in front of his gas station when a man in a pickup truck, intent on retaliation for September 11, shot and killed Sodhi, whom he assumed was Muslim. Sodhi wore a turban in honor of his Sikh faith. It was the first hate crime attributed to the aftermath of 9/11. The killer went on a spree that day, also shooting at an Afghan couple and a Lebanese man, and while being arrested, he said, "I'm a patriot and American. How can you arrest me and let the terrorists run wild?"

On the fifteenth anniversary of Balbir Singh Sodhi's death, his brother Rana made a phone call to the killer, who is serving a life sentence in jail. Rana Singh Sodhi forgave the killer, telling him that hate does not align with his beliefs and that he hoped he would be released so that he could educate other Americans about the destructiveness of discrimination. His aim is one of inclusiveness. In 2018, when speaking about his brother, Rana Singh Sodhi told CNN, "Who's American? We're all immigrant[s]. This is the land of immigrant[s]. This is the beauty of this country, we [are] all welcome with all different faiths, color, creed, and gender. . . . This is our responsibility to maintain, to make sure that this beauty, we keep it for every generation." Rana Singh Sodhi is not looking to go back—he is looking at moving forward, together, with all of us.

## IV. COVID-19: Isolation and Global Connection

Since the early months of 2020, the world has struggled to end a global pandemic, the likes of which we have not seen for over one hundred years. COVID-19 has affected every single country on the globe, and it has changed the ways that humans have gathered, interacted, and moved. The virus has developed several variants, and each continues to move across the world in waves; the virus does not heed human-made borders.

This halting moment in history has impacted every industry and every school. It has affected everything from government legislation to the way we buy our food. The isolation of quarantine has taught us a lot about what it takes to be apart from other humans.

The coronavirus pandemic also affected the scope, scale,

and methods of immigration to the United States. With increases in forces like climate change, global violence, and various pandemic-related crises and disasters, the need for many to migrate was strong, especially for asylum seekers. But the road to arrive has been much harder. At the pandemic's start in 2020, the United States began restricting travel. Some states banned nonessential travel. And in an attempt to secure borders, border patrol officials were given authorization to immediately deport undocumented individuals and asylum seekers—eradicating the right to due process. Immigration hearings were halted and the issuance of green cards was suspended. Refugee resettlement all but stopped, as the State Department announced it would allow the lowest number of refugees into the country in decades. All this, in the midst of a global crisis.

How was the United States able to pass and put into law so swiftly such severe legislation? It comes down to a similar strain of anti-immigrant rhetoric that weaves through many chapters in this book, and how that rhetoric intersected with current patterns of global migration. In the following chapter, we will look at just some of the innumerable policies passed in the last twenty years that have affected immigrants and newcomers. As we read these stories, it's important to remember that they are not over yet—they are ever changing, and their impact on our country will only become clearer in the future. Most importantly, it is important to remember the people—our neighbors—who are at the center of these stories. That we are, as John Lewis said, "one family. We all live in the same house."

## V. A More Welcome Way Forward

The history of immigration's link to discrimination begs the question: What can we change in order to curb this pattern? When thinking of how new immigrants often sprout up in the solidarity and the safety of common community, how might we, as their neighbors, do a better job of welcoming them into our spaces and our daily lives? Perhaps it's about daily interactions infused with welcoming, rather than ones led by division and hatred. Perhaps it's in recognizing, as Rana Singh Sodhi does, that this welcoming is our responsibility, as Americans, to maintain—through this wave of immigration and those in the future.

## LET'S TALK ABOUT IT

* What ways can you think of welcoming newcomers to your school, your block, or your community?

* Have you ever experienced a feeling of otherness? How did it come about? How did it make you feel? What made you feel better?

* Have any communities that you are a part of been discriminated against, or have you ever seen or heard messages of discrimination toward members of your community? What are ways you can work against those messages to welcome and include folks, including new immigrants who may have faced discrimination?

# CHAPTER 8
## AMERICA'S FUTURE

It wasn't until well after the civil rights movement that the United States began to see an increased number of Black immigrants arriving from elsewhere around the world. In 1980, the census counted 816,000 Black immigrants—that number increased to 2.4 million by 2000 and to 4.2 million in 2016. Large numbers of Black Americans today have immigrant origins or were immigrants themselves. Some have emigrated from countries in South America and Central America, while others have come from countries in Africa. Still others have made their journey from the Middle East and Europe. The largest Black immigrant population continues to originate from the Caribbean.

## II. Black Immigration Today

As the Institute for Caribbean Studies reminds us, "Caribbean immigrants have been contributing to the well-being of American society since its founding." Because the Caribbean was colonized by many of the same countries who fought over the lands that would eventually be the United States, the connections and pathways of movement between peoples of the Caribbean and America are strong. Prominent members of American culture like Vice President Kamala Harris, politician Shirley Chisholm, actor Sidney Poitier, and musician and entrepreneur Robyn Rihanna Fenty were all born in the Caribbean or born to Caribbean parentage. Nearly 50 percent of Black immigrants to America come from the Caribbean, from countries including Jamaica, Haiti, and the Dominican Republic. Many of these immigrants face racial discrimination when they arrive, and the United States has a long history of racist policies toward Haitian immigrants. Afro-Caribbean communities exist predominately in the northeastern United States and Florida, with other communities all over the country.

However, in the last forty years, immigration from African countries has flourished as well. Writer April Gordon refers to it as the "new diaspora." The last eight years have seen an increased number of communities from Ghana, Nigeria, and other sub-Saharan African countries moving to America—the population of sub-Saharan immigrants has increased 52 percent in this time period. Black immigrants from African countries have sprouted communities in states like California, Minnesota, Georgia, Texas, and New York. These increasing movements suggest a sea change in this slowly arriving population. A data company called the Pew Research Center predicts that by 2060, the Black immigrant population in the United States will nearly double.

Sometimes African immigrants travel first to Brazil or other South American countries and then make a very long, harrowing trek up to North America. A particularly dangerous part of their journey is through what's known as the Darién Gap, which runs from Colombia to Panama, linking South America to North America. Three quarters of the immigrants who make this journey on foot through remote rain forest are from Cuba and Haiti, but there are increasing numbers of African immigrants taking this route.

Among the dangers: inhospitable jungles and rivers filled with rushing water and deadly wildlife, and human bandits and kidnappers who prey on the refugees.

Often, once arriving to the United States, Black immigrants find themselves struggling with America's pervasive anti-Black racism. Former President Trump once queried why the United States needed immigrants from places like Haiti and African countries, using a derogatory term in reference to those places. In the same sentiment, he vocalized his wish that immigrants came to America from predominantly white countries like Norway. This sentiment, which was publicly denounced by the UN human rights office, is a dehumanizing one—one that assumes immigrants from some parts of the world are preferred to others. And this kind of thought makes its way, insidiously, down from the halls of power and into the day-to-day lives of the immigrants it affects. Black immigrants are often subject to anti-Black racism in their work and daily lives. According to the Immigrant Learning Center, "Immigrants are actually less likely than U.S.-born people to commit a crime, but immigrants of color are still more likely to become involved with the criminal justice system." Black immigrants make, on average, $8,000 less in yearly income than the average US household and $4,200 less than other US immigrant households. Black immigrants are more likely to be detained and deported on immigration issues than other immigrants, and their DACA applications are less likely to be approved.

Black immigrants in America are arriving to a country that has anti-Black racism in its history and its foundations. According to writer Isabel Wilkerson, Black immigrants are "exposed to the corrosive stereotypes of African-Americans and may work to make sure that people know that they are not of that group but are Jamaican or Grenadian or Ghanaian." It is something that exists in countries with roots in white supremacy—a tendency for oppressed and marginalized groups to pit themselves against one another for a seeming scarcity of resources. In the words of Yndia S. Lorick-Wilmot, each of these communities is contending with "a narrative of America wherein [B]lack voices and [B]lack personhood have no place within the context of and the participation in the American Dream." It will require all Americans to confront the reality of pervasive and insidious anti-Black racism in this country, as a first step toward changing biases that affect our Black immigrant populations.

As we have seen throughout this book, immigrant communities often turn toward one another for support and resources to build a better and more lasting future, living in proximity to one another, helping one another as they arrive here. This is true of Black immigrant communities, just as it is true of the Italian and Jewish communities who lived in the Lower East Side tenements, as it is true of the Chinese communities in San Francisco, as it is true of Latinx communities in Texas. One of these communities recently came into sharper focus. In the 1970s in the New York City borough of the Bronx, a Gambian immigrant named Abdoulie Touray moved to a building on East 181 Street. Upon his arrival, he opened the door to his apartment to any new immigrants from West Africa—to share a meal, read the Quran, share job opportunities, or even have a place to stay. The building became known as Touray Tower, and until recently it remained a central hub for immigrants and immigrant-descendant families from The Gambia and other countries in West Africa. Though Touray passed away in 2019, many Gambian families, including his own children and grandchildren, still lived in Touray Tower. In early 2022, the building caught fire, killing seventeen people and displacing members of this community. Following the tragedy, members of the local community came together to support the victims. Some volunteers at the Gambian Youth Organization helped collect donations while others delivered clothes, shoes, and food to shelters where displaced victims were living. As we learn about our immigrant histories, it is important to remember that communities—like the Gambian community of Touray Tower—are still actively working with one another to ensure better futures for our families—and that in the wake of such tragedies, they need good neighbors to steward them through. How might we ensure, as Americans, that our neighbors get the help they need in times of strife?

Black immigrants continue to arrive in America and work toward ensuring our country lives up to its promise. In the words of South African immigrant and comedian Trevor Noah, "We all deserve to achieve our fullest potential no matter where we come from."

### III. The Muslim Ban

Just weeks into 2017, and one week into President Trump's administration, an executive order was passed that called for an immediate ban in travel from seven predominantly Muslim countries. Many refugees who were arriving from war-torn countries, as well as visa-holding migrants, were barred entry into the United States—and those who were already on their way here were detained for hours at US airports. The ban against Muslim countries seemed to be an extension of long-brewing religious prejudice, which spanned many decades, from post-9/11 fear and xenophobia to stereotypes about the Middle East from the late twentieth century. The week the ban was announced, in my neighborhood in Queens, all the Yemeni delis went on strike and closed in protest. Thousands of protestors gathered at airports across the country, hoping to block the deportation of people being detained there. Because of protestors and lawyers for the American Civil Liberties Union, the forced deportations were halted. But elements of the travel ban remained in place, affecting travel for thousands of refugees, visa-holders, and even some naturalized citizens for the next several years.

## IV. The Power of Fear, the Power of Hate

What could cause such a dehumanizing law to be passed in the first place? Many of the policies enacted in the last few years have been driven by anti-immigrant rhetoric, much of it based in racist stereotypes and religious prejudice. This, as we've learned, carries precedent—based all the way back to the 1790 Naturalization Act, which promoted the immigration status of white Europeans while excluding everybody else. Often, the loudest anti-immigrant voices in the American fabric forget that their ancestors, at one point, were immigrants or newcomers to this nation. President Trump's grandfather, Friedrich Trump, was himself a German immigrant who arrived to America in 1885. In fact, all of the former president's grandparents, and even his mother, were immigrants.

When we engage in fear and hate of a perceived other, when we forget how similar our stories might be to others, we create an atmosphere of harm. It is the opposite of the "land of opportunity." In the face of hateful rhetoric, messages of acceptance and solidarity become only more powerful. Stories of hope rally us. Every peaceful protest that challenged these bans, separations, and deportations, every volunteer who stepped in to help these newcomers find their footing amid legal proceedings, and every voice that called out against these harmful policies was impactful.

## V. New Communities

Today, populations of refugee communities are revitalizing small towns across America. In 2021, when Afghanistan was overtaken by Taliban forces, an emergency exodus followed. Thousands of Afghans hoped to escape the Taliban's oppressive regime. In an article for *National Geographic*, writer Nina Strochlic chronicled the arrival of several Afghan refugees to Lancaster, Pennsylvania. Lancaster was founded by German Amish immigrants who were escaping religious persecution almost three hundred years ago. These neighboring refugee identities have found a solidarity with one another: They acknowledge and embrace their connection, as both moved to the United States under dire circumstances, striving for better and more equal lives, three hundred years apart.

Today the number of refugees allowed in the United States annually has increased, from 33,000 in 2017 to 125,000 expected in 2022. Lancaster, Pennsylvania, has been a landing pad for refugees from different areas in the world over many years: Refugees from Vietnam, Somalia, and Myanmar call Lancaster home. Similar refugee populations have been welcomed in Bowling Green, Kentucky, and Clarkston,

Georgia. Refugees who settle there start businesses, get involved in local grassroots movements, and work to welcome in the next group yearning to breathe free.

When Americans can embrace that pay-it-forward mentality, we may be able to overcome the exclusionary history of immigration in this country. When older and established immigrant communities can welcome those who are arriving now, with their words, their platforms, or their actions—we just might be able to live up to that American promise.

## VI. Looking Back to Go Forward

As we reflect back on the idea of the United States—a country founded on idealistic principles that are not necessarily equally doled out to all its citizens, or its prospective ones—it is important to remember the idea of shift and change. After all, only about 600 years ago, nonindigenous people began to arrive to North America with the aim to colonize it for its resources. Only 400 years ago, the first boat of enslaved Africans reached North American shores. Only 250 years ago, a group of settler colonists rebelled against the British crown with the attempt to establish a new independent nation. Only 174 years ago, the border on that nation was determined, and even then it has shifted and changed.

How can we learn from the mistakes of America's previous generations—and make our country welcoming to new tides? As climate change continues to shape and affect the Global South, the need and call for migration will continue to increase. Refugees and asylum seekers will continue to make sacrifices, set out on perilous journeys, and endanger themselves in the name of their futures. The challenges that befell past immigrants, and that current immigrants are facing now, will mirror the challenges of our immigrant future.

So how can we be malleable, how can we shift and change like the Rio Grande, to meet the needs of our neighbors? How can we prepare for this challenge—one that, like the pandemic, will shape the lives of not only Americans but also every human on Earth?

Robin Wall Kimmerer, a member of the Potawatomi Nation, is a writer, scholar, and professor who looks to nature to seek answers to humanity's toughest questions. In her book *Braiding Sweetgrass*, she writes about Indigenous stories: "I am a listener and have been listening to stories told around me for longer than I care to admit. I mean to honor my teachers by passing on the stories they have passed on to me." Perhaps by listening to this true history, by digging deeper to find more lost histories, we can honor those who lived before us. In writing this book, I pass on these stories to you.

We can start by listening—and looking hard—at the mistakes our country has made in the past. We can start by remembering that the future of our country was built on the promise of newcomers. The real history of this global movement centers around the people, whose wishes and dreams for a better life for themselves and their children calls them to embark on a great journey, filled with sacrifice and unknowns. That hope, for survival, for a better life, is what spurred so many immigrants toward our shores. It is that promise that America often fails to deliver on, that we continue to strive to realize.

The true history centers the humans who were affected and impacted by laws, prejudices, and the need to assimilate, in the same way they were aided by neighbors, volunteers, and their own communities. People who arrive here should learn the real history of the land they inhabit, the land of Indigenous North Americans, so that they may steward their new homes with intent to honor its first inhabitants.

It starts in small ways. Perhaps we shift our language, perhaps we shift our points of view. Perhaps we shift in larger ways, getting involved with local communities who might need assistance. By starting small and increasing ever so slightly, by remembering that each community is an important part of the larger whole, we might be able to change the narrative and the course of history.

Valeria Luiselli cites two lines in the Immigrant's Prayer in her book *Tell Me How It Ends*: "'Partir es morir un poco / Llegar nunca es llegar'—'To leave is to die a little / To arrive is never to arrive.'" Immigrants— alongside non-immigrants and Indigenous people—will continue to shape America's future. Once we recognize immigrants' role in this shaping, we can celebrate it. Once we believe it, we can work for it. Then, and only then, will America's promise be fulfilled. Only then will be truly arrive, together.

## LET'S TALK ABOUT IT

* What connections do you see between the way immigrants and refugees are treated today and the way they have been treated in the past? What patterns in history do you want to break?

# EPILOGUE
## A FINAL NOTE FROM JENNIFER SABIN, THE CREATOR OF TRUE HISTORY

There will always be people desperate to leave their countries, arriving to the United States with high hopes that the country will let them in and allow them to stay. As author Jaclyn Backhaus has already detailed throughout this book, there are many reasons that people flee their homes, for a country they've likely never seen, to start over. The countries of origin most represented in the immigration record might change from one generation to the next. But what doesn't change are the reasons human beings give up everything familiar to them to make a harrowing journey to the nation's borders or seek asylum through daunting bureaucratic systems; life as they've known it has become untenable. They dream of a life for themselves and their children that is safe from the threat of warfare, drug cartels, kidnappings, corrupt police states, and other threats of violence. They dream of a life that presents opportunities to enjoy a permanent roof over their heads, food on the table, and clean water. Some dream big and some dream simply of survival—but they all see a possible future in this country that has offered opportunities to so many millions of people before them.

What does not stay the same is this country's immigration policy. With each change in the White House, immigration laws and priorities change. Imagine how disconcerting it is to be a refugee, an asylum seeker, or a young adult with DACA status, knowing your fate could be directly tied to the next election. That was never so apparent as when President Donald Trump took office in 2017.

If we back up a bit, we must acknowledge that President Barack Obama (2009–2017) disappointed many people with his immigration policies: members of the immigrants-rights community who thought his policies would align more with their goals, and people on the other side of the issue who said he was too easy on unauthorized immigrants. While he instituted DACA, which shielded nearly eight hundred thousand young undocumented immigrants from being deported, Obama also deported more undocumented immigrants (three million) than any previous president, making noncitizens with criminal records and people who had recently crossed the US border illegally his top priorities for deportation. Some critics even called him the "Deporter in Chief."

Under President Trump, anti-immigrant policies and rhetoric ratcheted up significantly. And his zero-tolerance policy for illegal border crossings resulted in the child-separation policies that left so many children in detention centers as "unaccompanied minors" while their parents were detained in different facilities and prosecuted.

Trump was elected by and large on a platform that many people considered racist and anti-immigrant. You may remember he said, "When Mexico sends its people, they're not sending their best." He accused Mexican immigrants of being rapists, and he talked a lot about building a wall—a literal symbol to prevent them from entering the United States. Once President Trump took office, he wasted no time making it more difficult for very specific groups of people to find a home in the United States. For instance, on January 27, just days after his inauguration, he signed an executive order banning immigration from seven Muslim-majority countries. Trump's executive orders often targeted people with brown or black skin. In fact, he publicly mused that we should have more people coming here from Norway, rather than countries that he disparaged, like Haiti and El Salvador.

A man named Stephen Miller working in the Trump White House made it his mission to dismantle previous immigration policies and limit immigration as much as possible through travel bans. Miller accomplished this by significantly decreasing refugee numbers and by separating children from their parents. He also explored the possibility of limiting citizenship for legal immigrants. Ironically, Miller's own ancestors on his mother's side had immigrated to the United States in 1903 from what is now Belarus, escaping violent Russian anti-Jewish pogroms (organized massacres of particular ethnic groups). They were poor in Russia, and his great-great-uncle had only eight dollars in his pocket when he set foot on Ellis Island. But his family became prosperous, educated Americans, examples of the American dream. Miller's own uncle wrote that if they had not left Russia and immigrated to the United States, the family would likely have been murdered. Only seven of the two thousand Jewish citizens of the town they came from survived the Nazis.

How soon some people forget their own immigration story.

As a senior adviser to President Trump, Miller was instrumental in crafting ways to restrict immigration through formal rules that were public and, more quietly, through less-visible administrative actions. Sometimes one word on an immigration form would be changed—but it could result in an application being rejected on a technicality. One group of people tracking the changes to the immigration system found over a thousand changes made during the Trump Administration! Those changes often made it very difficult for immigration lawyers to keep up and help their clients. And in the end, Miller and the Trump Administration were quite successful in limiting immigration. For example, in 2016, President Obama approved 110,000 yearly spots for refugees. By 2020, President Trump cut that number down to fifteen thousand.

How immigration policy is transformed in the future is partly up to the voters. But as we've seen with the Obama Administration, it isn't always possible to predict exactly what is going to happen just because one party or the other is in office.

There is plenty of political posturing by politicians in both the Republican and Democratic Parties on the issue. When politicians perceive that immigration is a hot-button issue, as it was in the 2016 presidential election, they tend to jump into the fight and stake their claim on one side of the argument or the other to win votes. But these same politicians often lack realistic, comprehensive, and empathetic plans to overhaul US immigration policy. Often, their plans and attacks are reduced to quick, meaningless soundbites they hope will garner votes.

What does that mean for the future of immigration to the United States? It's difficult to know. The pressures on the United States to accept refugees will continue, and the numbers of those hoping to become Americans may increase dramatically. For example, we can predict that in the future, there will be more climate change refugees than we've ever seen before.

How old will you be in 2050?

One organization, the World Bank, predicts that by that year, there will be more than two hundred million people forced to leave their homes because of climate change. Millions of people will be compelled to find new homes because of water scarcity, decreasing crop productivity, rising sea levels, and unbearable air temperatures. Another study by the *Proceedings of the National Academy of Sciences* found that by 2070, one to three billion people could be living in places that are too hot for humans. Some cities and villages in the world are already considered too hot and too dry for human life. Where will all these climate refugees go?

Of course, the United States could never handle even a fraction of these climate refugees. And the United States may have some of its own problems: Parts of the United States will be less habitable due to climate change. But climate change will force Americans and their elected leaders to grapple with larger numbers of refugees seeking sanctuary in the United States. And it won't be just an American issue: The entire world will have to face these problems and figure out how to share and distribute resources.

In the meantime, citizens fleeing countries like Taliban-run Afghanistan, violent parts of Central America, and hurricane-ravaged Caribbean islands, to name a few, will continue to immigrate to the United States. Many of them will face deportation proceedings, abuse at the hands of ICE, and racism from US citizens and politicians who have short memories regarding their own family histories. These immigrants may have difficulty securing good jobs. They will face hardship on many fronts. Yet they will still leave their homes and travel very long distances to find new homes in this country.

Whether you think of the United States as a nation of immigrants or not, immigrants have always been intrinsic to the country's success and its vibrancy—and will continue to be so in the future. That is a legacy that no political party or president can ever unravel.

# SELECTED BIBLIOGRAPHY

Dunbar-Ortiz, Roxanne. *Not "A Nation of Immigrants": Settler Colonialism, White Supremacy, and a History of Erasure and Exclusion.* Boston: Beacon Press, 2021.

Hong, Cathy Park. *Minor Feelings: An Asian American Reckoning.* New York: One World, 2020.

*"Immigration and Relocation in U.S. History: Italian."* **Library of Congress.** *Immigration and Relocation in US History.* https://www.loc.gov/classroom-materials/immigration/italian/.

*"Irish-Catholic Immigration to America."* **Library of Congress.** *Immigration and Relocation in US History.* https://www.loc.gov/classroom-materials/immigration/irish/irish-catholic-immigration-to-america/.

Kimmerer, Robin Wall. *Braiding Sweetgrass: Indigenous Wisdom, Scientific Knowledge, and the Teachings of Plants.* Minneapolis: Milkweed Editions, 2013.

Liu, Zhaoyang. *"Pogroms and Russian Jewish Immigrants."* **Re-Imagining Migration.** https://reimaginingmigration.org/pogroms-and-russian-jewish-immigrants/.

Luiselli, Valeria. *Tell Me How It Ends: An Essay in Forty Questions.* Minneapolis: Coffee House Press, 2017.

Mehta, Suketu. *This Land is Our Land: An Immigrant's Manifesto.* New York: Macmillan, 2019.

Osborn, Carlyn. *"The Changing Mexico-U.S. Border."* **Library of Congress,** December 18, 2015. https://blogs.loc.gov/maps/2015/12/the-changing-mexico-u-s-border/.

Roberts, Alaina E. *I've Been Here All the While: Black Freedom on Native Land.* Philadelphia: University of Pennsylvania Press, 2021.

Wilkerson, Isabel. *Caste: The Origins of our Discontents.* New York: Penguin Random House, 2020.